Longman ex
practice kits

GCSE
English

Elizabeth A. Cripps

LONGMAN

Series Editors
Geoff Black and Stuart Wall

Titles available

GCSE	A-level
Biology	Biology
Business Studies	British and European Modern History
Chemistry	Business Studies
English	Chemistry
French	Economics
Geography	French
German	Geography
Higher Mathematics	German
Information Technology	Mathematics
Mathematics	Physics
Physics	Psychology
Science	Sociology

Addison Wesley Longman Ltd,
Edinburgh Gate, Harlow,
Essex CM20 2JE, England
and Associated Companies throughout the World.

First Published 1997
Second impression 1997

ISBN 0582-31191-8

British Library Cataloguing-in-Publication Data
A catalogue record for this book is available from the British Library.

Set in 11/13pt Baskerville
Produced by Longman Singapore Publishers Pte Ltd
Printed in Singapore

Contents

Acknowledgements

The Examination Boards mentioned in this book are thanked for their helpful replies to enquiries. I am particularly grateful to the following for giving permission to reproduce questions from their papers:

► London Examinations
► Northern Ireland Council for Curriculum, Examinations and Assessment
► Southern Examining Group

Permission has been granted to reproduce their questions. The answers or hints on answers (with the exception of those for Practice Paper A) are solely the responsibility of the author, and have not been provided or approved by the Groups.

I should like to thank colleagues and friends who have helped me in the preparation of this book and especially Mrs Caroline Footman, for advice on some of the oral material included, Miss Yvonne Clark for typing assistance and Mr Kenneth Uwah, librarian of The American College in London.

We are grateful to the following for permission to reproduce copyright material: *Belfast Telegraph* for an extract from an article by David Watson; the author, Zulfikar Ghose for his poem 'Geography Lesson' © Zulfikar Ghose, first published in *Jets From Orange* (Macmillan, London); the author's agent for an extract from *Fun City* by Barry Hines; Peterloo Poets for 'Half-past Two' by U.A. Fanthorpe from *Selected Poems*; *South London Guardian* for extracts from the articles 'Inferior sunglasses will ruin your eyes' and 'Ellen's climbing every mountain' from *Streatham & District 'Guardian'* edition 10.10.96; Walker Books Ltd for an extract from *Smokestack Lightning* by Laurence Staig, text © 1992 Laurence Staig.

How to use this book

This book is intended to help you to achieve the best grade you can in the GCSE English exams. As well as covering the essential topics common to all the exam boards, it provides helpful advice on the skills you need to tackle any type of English question. This is done partly by discussing students' answers and advising on how these would be assessed by the examining groups' marking schemes, and also by giving general advice from an examiner experienced in setting question papers and marking students' work.

The book is arranged in four parts.

Part I Preparing for the examination

Here you will find advice on planning your revision well ahead of the exam, using the enclosed Revision Planner. The different types of exam questions are illustrated, together with the skills and techniques needed for successfully answering each type.

It is vitally important that you understand the exam questions, so key words which are frequently used are listed and defined. This means that you can recognise at a glance what is required.

How you are marked is the next issue: this depends both on National Curriculum Attainment Targets, as well as the methods of each of the exam groups. These criteria are set out clearly so that you can become familiar with them before you take the exam.

Finally, your behaviour during exams can affect the result. To make the most of all your careful preparation, you can find out how to be ready to do your very best on the day.

Part II Topic areas and questions

There are five main modes of English examined:

- ▶ **Speaking and listening**
- ▶ **Reading comprehension**
- ▶ **Functional writing**
- ▶ **Creative writing**
- ▶ **Spelling, handwriting and presentation**

For each of these there are the following topic areas:

- ▶ **Speaking and listening: the individual oral**
- ▶ **Speaking and listening: paired and group orals**

- ▶ **Reading comprehension: literary text**
- ▶ **Reading comprehension: functional text**
- ▶ **Reading comprehension: media texts**

- ▶ **Writing: functional**
  - Diary writing
  - Directed summary writing
  - Letter writing
  - Newspaper article writing
  - Report writing
  - Speech writing

- ▶ **Writing: creative**
    - Descriptive writing
    - Dramatic writing
    - Imaginative writing
    - Narrative writing
    - Personal writing
    - Persuasive writing
- ▶ **Spelling, handwriting and presentation**

Within **each** of these topic areas you will find:

1 **Revision tips** Giving specific guidance on revising that particular topic area.
2 **Topic outlines** Briefly summarising the key skills you will need to practise in that topic area.
3 **Revision activities** To involve you actively in practising the topic area and checking your grasp of it.
4 **Practice questions** From recent papers or of the type you are likely to find in your exam.

It is important that you try to answer the questions before reading the answers provided in Part III of this book.

Part III Answers and grading

In this part there are answers sketched out by the examiner, indicating what assessors are looking for in each question. There are also answers written by students for each topic area. Each will have full notes to help you to identify both the qualities and the weaknesses.

There are also mark schemes and other guidance showing how examiners would award grades for answers, so that the qualities needed for higher grades are clear.

Part IV Timed practice questions with answers

Here there are parts of papers which will give you practice before the exam in timing yourself under exam-type conditions. Outline answers are provided so that you can compare your own performance, and see how well you have done.

PLANNING YOUR REVISION

▶ Revising English is more a matter of acquiring useful skills and brushing up what you know already than learning a great deal of new material. That should give you confidence. Do not become *over*-confident, though. Remember that you can always improve so as to present your skills in the best possible way.

▶ The first thing needed is to be sure what you have to do. Teachers and tutors will guide you about written papers but where coursework is involved make sure in good time that you have produced the required number of written pieces and the required range of styles. Also, prepare and do several pieces of speaking and listening work, so that your best can be selected for final assessment.

▶ Know what types of writing are required for the final written papers. If you have a weakness in any of these areas, concentrate on practising sample questions (of the kind found in this book and Longman's *Study Guide*).

▶ Some exam groups give out material in the form of theme booklets ahead of the exam. Get to know the pieces here well. Read them several times, choose the pieces you like best and try to work out questions that fit them.

▶ Some groups give you unseen reading comprehension tests. The best preparation for these is to read as much as you can during your course. Read different types of writing: newspaper articles, novels, short stories and poems to broaden your range.

▶ Learn to be *precise* in your reading. If you come across unfamiliar words, look them up in a dictionary and absorb them into your own vocabulary. If you come across words that you understand vaguely, look them up as well and get a clear focus on their meaning.

▶ Try writing brief summaries of material you read or lessons you are taught in class, in a rough workbook. Pick out the key ideas and aim to state them plainly and briefly.

▶ If you keep stopping and starting when you write, improve your fluency by keeping a diary – it could be a specialist diary about a hobby or interest. It really does help.

▶ If you have some favourite authors, try to analyse the way they put their books together and adopt some of their techniques for yourself.

▶ If you find it hard to think of interesting creative writing ideas, keep a writer's notebook for a year before the exam. Jot down plots, good ideas, interesting characters, memorable remarks – raw material for writing. This habit will make you more observant and alert to others' creative use of language.

▶ If you have a weakness in paragraphing, spelling or punctuation, *start to work on it very early*. Aim to do an hour two or three times a week, practising the skill, and make use of a book giving guidance (such as Longman's *Study Guide*).

▶ Most exam groups ask questions drawn from the media. Look closely at advertisements and newspaper articles and notice how they are structured, how words are used to entertain and persuade readers. Adopt some of these same techniques for yourself.

▶ You can learn a great deal that is useful for Speaking and Listening from watching television debates. Notice people's non-verbal communication or body language and how it helps or hinders their speech. In what ways do the most effective speakers present their message? You can be learning while relaxing watching television – honestly!

▶ Over the last three months before the exam, make use of the Revision Planner timetable which is in Part I of this book to practise areas of particular importance.

▶ Reading has been called 'sharing other peoples' minds and lives'. It is not just a chore but a maturing life experience. Try to enjoy it: you are growing while you study.

► Make sure you carry on having life experiences of your own besides school and study at home. They will make what you communicate more interesting and worthwhile.

► Remember: exam preparation is hard work and involves some sacrifice, but it is worth it for your future.

USING EXAM QUESTIONS IN REVISION

While you are revising a topic area, it is important that you look very carefully at the exam questions of the type you will find in your exam. (You will find some in Parts II and IV of this book and you should try them before looking at the answers in Parts III and IV.)

► Doing questions for yourself makes revision a positive activity.

► You will become more familiar with the type of language used in exam questions (see the list below, page 5).

► You will become much more aware of the differences between your effort and that of the examiner, or the answers of other students.

► Checking against the outline answers provided in Parts III and IV of this book will help you to see what the examiner was looking for.

► Comparing your answers with those of other students will help you to see your own strengths and weaknesses.

► Practising answering questions in the set time will help you to time your papers correctly in the exam. (You will find sample exam papers in Part IV of this book.)

TYPES OF EXAM QUESTIONS

► There is a greater variety of question types for English than for most other subjects in GCSE. You will not be asked to answer all of these types, but you should be prepared to do so, because any of them could appear in your exam.

► The first main distinction is between questions which you are asked to answer using *material given to you either before or during the exam* and those where you have to *provide everything from your own imagination*.

Questions based on material supplied by the examiner

► For this type it is important to read the material you are given – if it is a written text – very carefully once before looking at the questions and then again, searching for relevant material for your answer.

► If the material is a stimulus for speaking and listening, spend a little time sorting out how you react to it, what ideas and opinions you have about it and how you can shape a response to make your reactions clear to another speaker, the examiner and the audience or listeners. Be prepared to answer follow-up questions, too.

► Relevance is very important. Take particular care to find out from the wording of the questions whether the material may be used as a stimulus or 'jumping-off point' for you to use your own ideas, or whether you should draw ideas only from the passage/s. Every year many candidates confuse the instructions and so lose marks.

► If you are to base your answers only on the passage/s *be precise* in your reference to it. Don't misread the names of the characters, misspell key words that keep occurring in the text in front of you: many candidates lose marks by doing this, and it is so easy to avoid.

▶ If the texts are provided in a theme booklet ahead of the exam, spend plenty of time getting to know them well. Read and discuss the texts with other people, choose pieces you like and would hope to answer questions about if invited, and even think about what kind of questions are likely.

Questions based on your own ideas

▶ Here you have more to do, in one way, as you have to think about your own material and how to organise it into an answer. So spend several minutes planning, writing a flowchart, mind map or even listing ideas you want to include as a checklist. It is useful to glance back at it if you run out of things to write later.

▶ Keep to the point. Even imaginative writing is better if it has a definite focus. Do not leave your reader struggling to grasp your meaning, but give plenty of signposts as to your direction.

▶ Select the best possible mode or genre of writing, if you have a free choice. If one is given, e.g. write in diary or report form, make sure you know how to set this out appropriately and write in a suitable style. Some marks are always awarded for this.

Tasks for Speaking and Listening

▶ Read the instructions and set material (if any) steadily and be aware of the time set for the task. Do not just keep talking because you are nervous.

▶ Stay aware of your audience. Watch their body language. Are they bored? If so, adapt what you are saying to include and interest them. Remember that a speaker must communicate in a way that involves listeners.

▶ If you panic or go wrong, politely ask if you may begin again and do so, after taking a few deep breaths.

Written coursework tasks

▶ Make sure how many pieces you should include and what range of modes or genres should be included.

▶ Include some draft material, to show how the writing has evolved.

▶ Include some self-evaluation, explaining how you went about the writing, how successful you think it is and how you would tackle it differently, with hindsight.

▶ Make sure that the details on the folder cover are all fully and correctly completed.

All questions

▶ Think carefully about the wording of the question. Notice or underline key phrases so that you will be sure to meet the requirements of the task.

▶ Don't be tempted to write on something you know better which is *roughly* on the same topic!

▶ Avoid trying out something smart or new: exams are the wrong place to experiment.

▶ If you are asked to write in *your own words*, avoid copying or repeating stretches of the original text.

▶ Plan your time carefully and make sure that you *answer all questions*. You will probably lose more marks by not finishing a paper than by doing all the answers not very well.

▶ Spend a few minutes thinking and planning. Written plans are looked at by the examiners if a student cannot finish an answer. They may give you a few more marks.

▶ If there are word limits, keep to them. Examiners usually count to make sure that students have not exceeded the limit and simply cross out excess writing.

▶ If the papers are in two tiers, or levels, make sure you have the right one.

▶ Check how many questions or parts of questions you have to answer and do not do too few or too many. Also look at all the pages of the paper. It may seem obvious, but sometimes nervous students miss a whole page.

▶ Remember that examiners practise *positive marking*. They want to reward you for all that you *can* do!

NB Skills and techniques for each of the modes of Reading, Writing, Speaking and Listening will also be discussed in Part II: The topic areas.

COMMAND WORDS USED IN EXAM QUESTIONS

Analyse   Break into separate parts and discuss, or interpret each part.

Assess   Make an informed judgement about something, weighing up the strengths and weaknesses, or pros and cons.

Compare   Examine two or more things, and pick out their similarities.

Consider   Give opinions in relation to given information.

Contrast   Examine two or more things and pick out the differences.

Criticise   Make judgements; also give details to support your views.

Debate   Consider both sides of the question and come to a conclusion.

Define   Give the meaning, or precise limits, of the topic.

Describe   Give a detailed account of qualities, parts, etc.

Discuss   Consider both sides of an issue; maybe compare and contrast, or focus on their differences.

Distinguish between   Show the differences between two aspects or accounts, descriptively or critically.

Enumerate   List several ideas, aspects, reasons, qualities.

Evaluate   Give your opinion or refer to those of critics. Include evidence, quotation, details in support.

Examine   Give a detailed description or critical account of the topic.

Explain   Make an idea clear; show logical development with reasons.

Illustrate   Give major examples. Explain through examples, featuring them centrally.

Interpret   Explain the meaning of a text.

Outline   Give all the main ideas: an overview of the subject.

Prove   Support fully with facts.

Relate   Show the connection between ideas and/or place them against broader relevant issues.

Review   Go back briefly over earlier points.

Sketch   Give main ideas briefly.

State   Explain precisely.

Summarise   Give a brief version, avoiding unnecessary details.

Trace   Show how events or arguments progress and develop.

ASSESSMENT OBJECTIVES IN ENGLISH

All syllabuses are based on and closely reflect the Attainment Targets and Programmes of Study set out in the National Curriculum for English. Each area has Attainment Targets, referred to as an **ATs**.

For English, the **ATs** are:

AT1 Speaking and Listening
You must show in conversation and discussion that you can:

- speak about personal experience, giving your views and feelings
- discuss in groups, expressing your own ideas and listening to those of others
- give information and explain clearly
- work in a group to plan and give a presentation
- show you understand that how you speak may change, depending on your listeners and your purpose

You can meet these aims by working at activities including giving instructions, problem-solving, making a group presentation, debating and putting forward an argument. You should make some use of standard English.

AT2 Reading
You must show that you can read a variety of books, plays, poems, articles, both fiction and non-fiction:

- confidently and correctly
- showing that you respond to thoughts and feelings
- showing that you have read media articles and understand how they are written to meet a certain purpose
- take information from various texts and make use of it
- understand how styles of writing differ

You can meet these aims by reading widely both twentieth-century texts and some earlier ones, including Shakespeare. Learn to discuss these and form your own opinions about them. Vary your own reading methods, sometimes reading quickly to get a general impression, and sometimes reading and re-reading carefully for critical study.

AT3 Writing
You must show that you can:

- write in different ways for different purposes
- write in paragraphs and with correct punctuation
- choose suitable vocabulary for the purpose
- edit, proofread and self-correct your writing

AT4 Presentation
You must show in your writing that you can:

- spell words which are frequently used
- write clearly and lay out your work attractively

You can meet these aims by writing in a variety of ways, such as diaries, letters, reports, reviews, and newspaper articles. You could also try some stories, poems and dramatic scripts.

DURING THE EXAM

It is a pity to spend a great deal of time preparing carefully for the exam and then not do your very best on the actual day. Here are a few points to bear in mind:

► Go to bed early the night before and have a good night's sleep. Freshness and energy in the exam is very important.

► Have a good breakfast and set off really early. If your bus or train is held up, you need not panic.

► Take your card with your candidate number on it.

► When you get your paper, make sure it is the correct level or tier.

► Read the instructions and check how many questions you should answer.

► Notice how many marks are given for each question and make sure you complete those with most marks. Those with only a few marks require short answers, but the rest need longer answers.

► Spend a few minutes thinking about and planning each question. Don't think you have to keep writing *all* the time. Don't be unsettled by someone nearby who seems to have covered twice as many sheets of paper as you have. Remember, *quality is more important than quantity!*

► If there are passages to be read, settle down and read them once or twice before you answer any questions.

► Make sure that you have turned over *all* pages of the paper.

► Make sure that you use your time carefully so that you do complete the paper.

► Try to leave a few minutes at the end of the exam to read through and self-correct what you have written.

Then you will know that you have really done your best.

part II
Topic areas and questions

Speaking and listening: the individual oral

All exam groups will expect you to have fulfilled the aims set out in the National Curriculum **ATs** for Speaking and Listening (see page 6). Check these over with your teacher and make sure that your oral work is appropriate and sufficient. Oral assessment will take place throughout your course either by your teacher and/or an external assessor. Sometimes a video recording will be made that can be sent to the exam group as part of the exam.

It is important that you prepare carefully beforehand so that you are not too nervous. These are the points you should practise:

▶ Your speech should be clear and audible. It does not matter if you speak with a regional dialect, as long as you can be heard and understood.
▶ Your speech should not be too hurried. Sometimes during oral tests candidates get quicker and quicker, anxious to get it over and done with! Avoid this happening by pausing at suitable moments, taking a deep breath and counting to three silently, before continuing.
▶ Try not to fidget or wave your hands about.
▶ Even if you are reading a passage, or giving a short set talk, remember to look up often at your listeners.
▶ Find out how much time you have and practise beforehand, so that your talk will fit.
▶ Don't try to communicate too much when giving a point of view – two or three clear ideas expressed will be enough.
▶ Talk, like writing, needs a shape. Let your listener know when you are beginning, give some signals as to what order things will progress in and conclude pleasantly.
▶ Talk fluently. If you 'dry up', pause, then start that part of the talk again.
▶ If you are giving a talk, have a few reminder points on cards, then keep your head up and speak confidently, glancing down now and then. Do *not* read continuously with your head down.
▶ Try to combine specific information with your own opinion.
▶ If you have any visual aids, put them up securely. Make use of them by referring to them as you talk.
▶ Sound interested and lively, then you are likely to interest your listeners.
▶ Answer questions pleasantly and constructively.
▶ Conclude the oral pleasantly, with thanks.

Individual oral work covers three main aims in the **ATs**:

▶ to show that you can talk about personal experiences, expressing your views and feelings (**AT.2**)
▶ to offer information and explain something to an assessor/teacher (**AT.3**)
▶ to be aware, while you are talking, of your listeners and communicate suitably to keep them interested and involved (**AT.5**)

Talking about personal experiences

The three golden rules for any piece of individual oral work are:

1 **Be clear and intelligible**
2 **Be aware all the time of your listeners and try to hold their interest**
3 **Be well-organised**

Sometimes, talking about personal experiences will involve your feelings. That is only to be expected and is quite appropriate – but don't get 'carried away' so that you talk too much, or lose control of what you are saying.

The best way to make sure you are heard is to talk as if you were addressing someone at the back of the room, without increasing your volume to a level that your listeners find uncomfortable. There's no need to shout!

Look up. Don't cover your face by holding a piece of paper in front of you.

Listeners let you know how they are responding to your talk through their non-verbal communication: looking down, closing their eyes, looking at the clock! They may cough, fidget, yawn or look anxious for you. You want them to be relaxed. The best way, besides being heard, to hold your listeners' interest, is to have your talk well planned.

Have a definite beginning:

> Good morning/afternoon. My name is . . . and I'm going to give my impressions of a recent job experience.

Next, give advance warning of how your talk will proceed:

> I want to start with the interview, then go on to how I managed on the first morning, and finish with how I felt, looking back over the experience.

Your listeners will be glad to have some **signposts** to remind them of your structure and encourage them to keep listening:

> Mr Green, our careers teacher, arranged an interview for me . . .

> Well, that first morning! I got there half-an-hour late because roadworks held up the bus . . .

> Looking back, I felt quite sad to leave because . . .

After that, don't just sit down, looking relieved, giggle or say 'That's it'. Conclude by saying:

> Thank you for listening. I hope I've managed to give you a good idea of what the experience was like

or something similar.

Offering information and explaining something

The **three golden rules** mentioned above still apply but the last is probably all-important here. You can underestimate how easy it is to explain something clearly to someone else. Think of the last time you gave directions to someone who stopped you in the street and asked you the way. The better *you* know how to do something, the less it seems necessary to tell someone else all the details about it. This is known as *assuming too much knowledge*.

You will probably have some kind of stimulus material. It could be a diagram or a request to give instructions. If so, look at it carefully and mentally plan your answer step by step. Remember to have a clear first stage, signposts for each subsequent stage and a definite point of conclusion:

> Before taking a bungee jump, you need a medical checkup to ensure that you are fully fit, and your parents' permission, if you are under eighteen . . .

Then, wear suitable sports gear and . . .

You will be given an order in the line-up of jumps . . .

and so forth until

And finally, when it's all over, you'll feel a wonderful sense of elation and achievement as your signed certificate is put in your hand.

Do not write out the whole talk. Have key points written on index cards that you can hold in one hand and glance at when necessary.

If you are providing any visual aid, make use of it actively. Refer to it by combining general statements, with specific examples:

Bungee jumps don't take place just anywhere. This diagram of Chelsea Bridge shows the position where jumpers stand. As you can see, it is clear of any obstructions so, in that way, it is quite safe

or

Here is a certificate showing the type of jumps you can attempt.

Record of jumps

Swallow dive	1	2	3		Name		
Back flip	★	★	3		Club membership number		
Blindfold	1	2	3		. . . .		
Tandem	★	2	3		Expiry date		
Somersault	★	★	★	★	★		
Straight jacket	★	2	3			Photo	
Bridge jump	1	2	3			of you	
Super jump	★	★	3			jumping	

Figure 1
The types of jumps attempted

Invite questions at the end and be ready with answers. You can feel that you are the 'expert' if you really know your subject. It is a good feeling to have helped someone else understand something you have taught them.

Being a listener

Part of your assessment will be how well you listen to others: communication is a two-way process and some exam groups (e.g. **NICCEA**) emphasise this.

To be a good listener you should concentrate, follow in your mind and silently respond to what is said. Think of some questions to ask. React emotionally, showing humour, sympathy, interest, surprise or dismay as appropriate. Don't sit with a frozen expression: encourage the speaker by looking interested and involved.

REVISION ACTIVITY

This activity is to help you to meet the **AT** for the individual oral in **Speaking and Listening**.

Prepare a ten-minute talk on a sporting activity you know well. Explain how it works, what kind of pleasure you get from taking part in it or watching it and what kind of national or international standards and achievements have been reached. Try to include some illustrative material, such as diagrams, videoclips, pictures or actual sporting equipment necessary for anyone taking part. Then give the talk to a person whose judgement you trust. Using the chart on page 13, evaluate your own performance after a trial run, then ask your

		Yes	*No*
1	Is speech clear and audible?	☐	☐
2	Does the talk have a good opening?	☐	☐
3	Is speech properly paced?	☐	☐
4	Is there any distracting body language?	☐	☐
5	Is the speaker aware of listeners?	☐	☐
6	Is the talk too long?	☐	☐
7	Has the main theme been made clear?	☐	☐
8	Does the talk have a plan?	☐	☐
9	Is the speaker fluent, not hesitant?	☐	☐
10	Are the speaker's own ideas and feelings given?	☐	☐
11	Are examples and visual aids well managed?	☐	☐
12	Does the speaker sound interested?	☐	☐
13	Was the speech concluded well?	☐	☐
14	Did the speaker invite questions?	☐	☐
15	Were the questions answered well?	☐	☐

Figure 2
Individual oral
evaluation chart

listener to make an independent evaluation, using the same chart. Compare the two results.

PRACTICE QUESTIONS

There is considerable diversity in the type of tasks the different examining groups recommend.

For **London Examinations** you are advised to prepare an individual talk or engage in some role-play (this is discussed below under Paired Orals pages 15–17). Here are tasks of the kind set.

Question 1
Give your views on advertisements which shock.

Question 2
Give your views on the nuclear disarmament issue.

Question 3
Give your views on an item currently in the news.

Question 4
The National Lottery has been set up to provide money for charitable organisations. Your task is to make a bid for some of this money. You are to provide an interviewing panel with the aims and objectives of those you represent, together with a simple outline of the project and its cost. Make an oral submission of some 4–5 minutes in support of your bid. Be prepared for the panel to question you.

For **MEG** you may be asked to give a personal account of something, read aloud or describe something you have heard or seen.

Question 5
You might choose to read something from a text you are studying in class, for example a few paragraphs from a novel or a short story.

Question 6
You might describe attending a recent concert.

NEAB requires you to talk about texts you have read. This relates to **AT1.5 Knowledge about Language** which is to show that you have an understanding of how style varies, depending on its purpose and the type of reader or listener.

NICCEA emphasises that you will be assessed as a **listener** as well as a speaker. Out of the **four tasks** required, you may be asked to read a text aloud, give or listen to a formal presentation, or a debating speech.

SEG will want you to read and show response to a work of fiction for an individual oral or give a talk focused on how language is used for different purposes. Here are two likely tasks:

1 Give a five-minute talk evaluating an extract quoted in the theme booklet *Places* (set 1995) and illustrate your talk with quotations read from the text.
2 Interview one of the people in the booklet for a radio programme called 'People and Places'.

WJEC asks you to perform tasks similar to those outlined above.

2 Speaking and listening: paired and group orals

REVISION TIPS

Here you need to work with others, so bear the following points in mind:

- It will be important to be in a group where you feel you can talk comfortably.
- Sometimes in group discussions one or two students say very little, even nothing at all. If this is your problem, talk about it with your teacher or tutor and try to work in a small group with friends.
- Alternatively, some students dominate every group, talking loudly all the time. If this is your problem, remember that an assessor will not be impressed. Group work involves listening to and including others.
- Discussion is unpredictable and may get heated. If this starts to happen, keep cool. Remember that people who make major decisions about human problems need a clear head. **Light** not **heat** is what others respect.
- In a discussion pair or group, being well-informed is important. Support your argument with a strong, accurate piece of information.
- You should try to take a turn as leader or initiator of the talk. In this situation, also help others to speak.
- If role-play is involved, keep in character. Think yourself into the character and use suitable expressions as well as a tone and/or accent.
- Watch TV discussion programmes and notice the skills of successful chair persons and participants.

TOPIC OUTLINE

Paired and group oral work covers three main aims in the **ATs**:

- you should show that you can share and exchange views and ideas with others (**AT1.2**)
- you should be able to plan and take part in group presentations (**AT1.4**)
- you should be able to show that speech varies according to situation, purpose and listeners (**AT1.5**)

Exchanging views with others

You will need more or less the same basic communication skills as those mentioned above for the individual oral.

The first two golden rules:

1 **Be clear and intelligible**
2 **Be aware all the time of your listeners and try to keep their interest**

are still vital.

The third rule could be changed to:

3 **Be well informed**

and a fourth rule added:

4 **Be tolerant of others' views**

Your level of fluency may differ from that in the individual oral if you were giving a prepared talk. In spontaneous discussion it is natural to hesitate, to think about an idea, to repeat yourself when putting a point across. Don't try to 'talk like a book'! The earlier third rule '**be well-organised**' can work against you if you are not aware that it may. Students who have pre-planned what they want to say may be at a disadvantage. You need to respond quickly to changes of direction in the discussion, be prepared to react thoughtfully to new ideas, and defend or modify your earlier view, as necessary.

We all know the type of person in radio phone-ins who has one view and keeps repeating it until the host fades the caller out. If you are sincere in holding a view and wish to defend it, then you should take into account the arguments that others are putting forward: that will make your own defence stronger and more convincing.

The person who *does* need to be well-organised is the leader or initiator of a group discussion. It is his or her job to add new information to change direction if the talk goes dead, to add information to back up someone's point, to introduce the discussion by clearly stating the issue and to end it by summing up the main ideas put forward and the consensus reached.

As a participant in group discussion, one of the hardest things to achieve is to listen tolerantly to the views of others when you don't agree with them. It is easy to become scornful and dismissive of ideas you don't share – but it is more mature to listen politely, then try to undermine them with calm reasoning.

Plan and take part in group presentations

Most of the skills mentioned above are relevant here. More group-planning and discipline is involved, though. You need to decide who does what and ensure that each person has made thorough preparations. Balance your own role with flexibility, especially when answering questions at the end.

Show that speech varies according to situation, purpose and listeners

Probably the best way to demonstrate this is through role-play. If you are involved in role-play, take a few minutes to think yourself into the role first. Then try to sustain the expressions, tone and perhaps accent of the character you are taking on.

REVISION ACTIVITY

This activity is to help you to meet the aims of the **ATs** for the paired and group orals.

Senior pupils in school have the use of a pleasant Common Room where they can relax, play music and have snacks. One afternoon a group of unidentified pupils has come in and vandalised the room, painting graffiti on the walls and damaging some of the furniture. Take part in a group discussion involving the roles of head teacher, head of Senior School, head boy or girl, school caretaker and several senior pupils. Outline the problem and talk through the ways of solving it.

Arrange to have a group of listeners, and possibly record the discussion on audiotape or video. (Remember that recordings make some people feel inhibited. If you have to submit one, practise in front of the camera or listen to your recorded voice beforehand.) Let the listeners give feedback about the discussion covering the following points:

		Yes	No
1	Was there a leader of the group?	☐	☐
2	Did he or she introduce the topic well?	☐	☐
3	Did he or she control the speakers?	☐	☐
4	Was anyone inaudible?	☐	☐
5	Did anyone talk too much?	☐	☐
6	Did the discussion keep going?	☐	☐
7	Did everyone keep 'in role'?	☐	☐
8	Did anyone go off the point?	☐	☐
9	Was there any distracting body language?	☐	☐
10	Did the leader sum up effectively?	☐	☐

Figure 3
Group oral chart

PRACTICE QUESTIONS

London Examinations recommends three areas for work: group discussion, problem-solving in pairs and role-play. Here is a recent question:

1 Your parents have gone away for the weekend, leaving you in charge. A noisy party is held and some damage is done to the flat. The police are called because of complaints by neighbours.

(a) With a partner, role-play the following:

    1 the conversation you have with the police officer

    2 the conversation you have with the trouble-makers after the police have left

    3 the conversation you have with your parents, when they return home

(b) With your partner, discuss the styles of speech you used in each conversation. What kind of language and expression did you employ in the different situations? Why was the type of spoken English you used appropriate to the situation?

SEG similarly requires a task focused on discussion about language use but also, like **MEG**, suggests a collaborative group activity or one involving the interaction of pairs.

    NEAB recommends talk to a variety of audiences: small group discussion and whole-class discussion.

    NICCEA offers the example of formal role-play and informal role-play as well, showing that you can hypothesise and speculate.

    Typical tasks given are:

1 Give a five-minute news broadcast for the BBC.

2 Act as narrator telling a story as an old person looking back on an early memory of youth.

WJEC also offers a range of very similar tasks.

3 Reading comprehension: literary text

This type of comprehension includes poetry as well as prose passages from fiction.

✓ REVISION TIPS

Comprehension tests are of two kinds:

► unseen
► using prereleased tests

Unseen

The reading will be new to you and will be set on the exam paper. The best way to prepare is to gain as much reading experience as you can during your GCSE years of study. Read a wide variety of material: stories, novels, plays and poems for enjoyment but also notice how writers achieve their impact. What do you like about the style? Also, learn to be a focused reader: if you come across words and phrases that you do not understand, or only grasp vaguely, look them up at a convenient time and remember them.

Using prereleased texts

Most exam groups offer theme booklets of prereleased texts. These will be given out a short time before the exam for you to read and think about. If you receive one of these, do as advised above, and also concentrate on the texts that particularly interest you or that you enjoy. Get to know them really well.

⊙ TOPIC OUTLINE

The aims you should try to succeed in as set out in the **ATs** are to show that you can:

► read confidently and understand a variety of texts (**AT2.1**)
► respond to literature (fiction, poetry, drama) (**AT1.2**)
► appreciate how writers use language (**AT1.5**)

You should also be able to make critical judgements about what you read and support your points by referring back to the text.

Comprehension questions are intended to test whether you understand what you are asked to read and can respond to its mood (or the feelings it gives most readers) and style.

The **five golden rules** here are:

1 **Read carefully**
2 **Answer relevantly**
3 **Look out for inference as well as for explicit meaning**
4 **Support your answer**
5 **Write clear, focused answers**

▶ Read the material once for general interest and enjoyment. Look over the questions, then read them again carefully, bearing them in mind.

▶ As you answer each question, check the text to make sure that you are being precise in your answer (unless you are asked to give your own ideas). Vary the length of your answers: those with one or two marks only need a few words or a sentence; others need longer answers, with more detail. Check the wording of the questions (see glossary of question commands on page 5). If you are asked to write in your own words, *do not repeat the words of the passage.* If you are asked to say what words in the passage mean, *try to be precise in your answer.* Sometimes you are asked to give your own ideas, or use the passage as a 'jumping-off' point for writing, for example in Question 3 below. If so, make sure that *the examiner can find some clear connection between the passage and your own answer.*

▶ The answers to some questions can be found by reading the text for its exact or explicit meaning, known as **reading the lines**, for example in Question 1 below. Others need you to work out the meaning for yourself from clues given in the text. This is known as **inferencing** or **reading between the lines**, for example in Question 2 below.

▶ Some comprehension questions want you to show your understanding by referring back to the text, for example in Question 2 below. This may be by quoting from it or by giving details in your own words. If you have not done this anywhere on your paper, you will lose marks.

▶ Although marks may not be taken off directly for poor grammar, spelling and punctuation, these things may make your answers unclear to the examiner. Be as correct as you can, and don't write too casually.

REVISION ACTIVITY

This exercise is intended to help you meet the aims mentioned above. (The questions are based on a poem in the prereleased material in the booklet *Places* (**SEG**).) First, read the poem several times, as if you had had time to do so before the exam.

Geography Lesson

When the jet sprang into the sky,
it was clear why the city
had developed the way it had,
seeing it scaled six inches to the mile.
There seemed an inevitability
about what on the ground had looked haphazard,
unplanned and without style
when the jet sprang into the sky.

When the jet reached ten thousand feet,
it was clear why the country
had cities where rivers ran
and why the valleys were populated;
the logic of geography –
that land and water attracted man –
was clearly delineated
when the jet reached ten thousand feet.

continued

> *continued*
>
> When the jet rose six miles high,
> it was clear that the earth was round
> and that it had more sea than land.
> But it was difficult to understand
> that the men on the earth found
> causes to hate each other, to build
> walls across cites and to kill.
> From that height, it was not clear why.
>
> *Zulfikar Ghose*

Now answer the following questions:

1   In each verse two things become clear to the poet. Explain, *with reference to the text*, what these are. [*8 marks*]

2   Explain, *in your own words*, what the title means here. [*2 marks*]

3   Imagine yourself in a plane. Write about what you see, what you think and what you like or dislike about being there. [*10 marks*]

PRACTICE QUESTIONS

You should spend about 15 minutes reading the following passage and thinking about the questions before you begin to write. The passage is taken from *Smokestack Lightning* by Laurence Staig. In this book, Laurence Staig writes about his experience of growing up in the 1960s.

My parents had made their minds up that when I went to secondary school they would try to move house again. They thought that I should have my own bedroom, not only because of studying, homework and so on, but simply because I was getting older. My mother had put our name down for a council house or flat, but there was an incredible waiting list that went into years.   *5*

As usual, my father left this side of things to my mother, and through an agency she found us a flat in Berwyn Road. We rented the upper floor of a 1920s semi-detached that appeared to be in the middle of being repaired. Everything was unfinished: the front garden wall looked as if the bricklayers had stopped for lunch; inside, the wallpaper only went round half of the walls and the odd door was   *10* painted with undercoat only. We should have heeded these signals, but my parents were desperate. My mother had been determined to escape from 321 Gothic Towers.

The accommodation was unfurnished, and the rent not too outrageous (rare in those days). It seemed that we had finally landed on our feet; we had found a   *15* 'normal' house. Except for a couple of details, such as having to share the bathroom with the landlord, whose name was Bert, and the kitchen being so small that our cooker had to be installed on the landing, it seemed a palace. Bert also had a cooker on the lower landing, one flight of stairs down, outside the bathroom. This was temporary, we were assured, and he was about to disconnect it.   *20*

Bert Westgate was, I suppose, in his late thirties, but he looked older. Lanky, with thinning hair, he had once been a professional footballer before a knee injury put an end to a sports career. He had the most strikingly bowed legs I had ever seen. Bert was a real lad. His trade was plastering (with some bricklaying).

Bert lived in the downstairs front room on his own. He slept on a pull-down   *25* couch. When we were shown around the house, he maintained that his life style was such that he ate out, or brought home fish and chips or a Chinese take-away, so he had no need of a kitchen. As we learned, the cooker outside the bathroom was *occasionally* used, and the dishes were *occasionally* left in the bathroom sink with Bert's socks, pants or shirts. **30**

A condition that we were able to move into Bert's house was that we gave him one hundred pounds rent in advance. Bert, we learned, had debts. My father put this down to the stresses and strains of life – didn't we all have debts, after all? One hundred pounds was a lot of money in those days, the rent was three pounds a week, so we were discussing almost two thirds of a year's advance. Bert's debts **35** were mainly gambling debts. Since my father also shared Bert's weakness for betting on the horses, he perfectly understood Bert's predicament.

Bert went through money as though he had his own Bank of England printing-press down in the cellar. He liked to go out and have a good time, and shortly after moving in, we witnessed the Bertrand Westgate smartening up ritual, which was to **40** accompany periods of short-term affluence.

One of the most dreadful things that we had to put up with was the massive fry-up on the landing, combined with the ritual of washing and shaving, while drying his socks above the grill. A tour down memory lane with his vocal cords followed: Bert went through all of Frank Sinatra's early songs, and an occasional song or two **45** (if we were lucky) from the current hit parade. Bert had a terrible voice, but to his ears it was a gift to be shared.

Bert hardly ever seemed to work. He was simply incredibly lazy. This explained the unfinished building projects about the house. The summer and spring months saw him reasonably active and he would try to rise by midday. When the winter months **50** arrived we discovered that he was really a dormouse, capable of spending an entire winter in bed. I thought this was extraordinary.

Towards the end of summer, I finally received the go-ahead from my parents concerning my lifelong ambition to own a dog (Bert had said he didn't object). I didn't care what dog it was, as long as it had a black shiny nose and barked. As we didn't **55** have much money the dog was going to have to cost next to nothing, and this ruled out a pedigree.

With the help of the People's Dispensary for Sick Animals I was given the address of some newly delivered mongrel puppies. I brought home a black and white mongrel, who I named Sally. She cost five shillings. **60**

When I presented the dog to my parents their first reaction was to stare at one another in disbelief. My father shook his head and said, 'My God, we've got another child in the house.'

Question 1

(a) Look closely at lines 1–30. Explain why Laurence and his family were pleased to move into their new flat in Berwyn Road. What early signs were there that there might be problems for them in their new home? [*10 marks*]

(b) What do you think about Bert? Referring to the passage, explain what his behaviour tells you about his character. [*10 marks*]

4 Reading comprehension: functional text

✓ **REVISION TIPS**

The best preparation for this type of reading is to become alert to the type of material of this kind that crops up in everyday life: forms to fill in, instructions for doing something, official letters and school handouts. The style of writing is much more business-like to fit the purpose. You will also be set texts of this kind for class and homework.

⊙ TOPIC OUTLINE

The **ATs** you need to reach here are:

▶ You should be able to understand how non-literary text is written and judge how well it communicates (**AT2.3**)
▶ You should be able to gather and plan so as to use information from functional texts in topic work (**AT2.4**)

Understanding and evaluating non-literary text

The **four golden rules** to remember here are:

1 **Read carefully**
2 **Answer relevantly**
3 **Take account of the purpose of the text**
4 **Answer in a suitable style**

▶ You may think that this kind of text is easier to read and understand than literary text, and often that is right. It is more likely to require **reading the lines** or **understanding explicit meaning**. The factual details are often vitally important, though, and careless reading may lead you into making more mistakes than you need, so take your time, and reread the text.
▶ Selecting the important points to answer the question is something that some students find difficult. If you do, draw a tree diagram. The trunk will show the main idea, the branches are the other clear arguments and the twigs are the examples, as shown in Figure 4.
▶ The purpose of the text may result in a particular layout, type of printing or use of illustration. Gather information, however it is presented to you.
▶ Your own answers should be in standard English and as direct and clear as you can make them. If you yourself are asked to use a particular style (for example, write a report or a letter) make sure that you use the proper layout and style, too. (See pages 29–38 for further advice on how to do this.)

Gathering information from functional text

▶ Read the text as you would any functional piece of writing. This will be a quick read, **scanning** the text for its main message.
▶ Then, **search reading** slowly and carefully, pick out the main idea, and the other clear points or arguments.

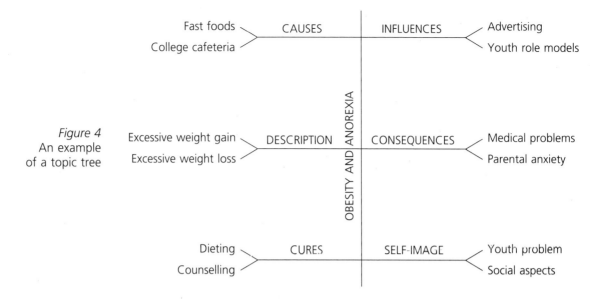

Figure 4
An example
of a topic tree

▶ You could underline these, or list them in note form. Put brackets round the details. The information in the text will then stand out clearly in front of you, from the most important to material of minor importance.

▶ Now look at the questions to see what information you have been asked to select. It will be easier to do this after your early preparations. Choose points for your answer.

▶ Rearrange them in the best order for the answer.

▶ Unless you are instructed otherwise, rewrite this information *in your own words*.

REVISION ACTIVITY

This activity is to help you practise the **ATs** mentioned above.

1 Read the passage below carefully, then answer the questions which follow.

The Blues

The Blues originated in America during the early years of the 1900s. No exact date is given to the first Blues song, nor was there a first person to play the Blues; in a sense, it was always there. Only in the 1920s was it recorded and sold, first in America and then throughout the world.

The Blues is a form of music that expresses a sadness in its notes and was played originally by many negro slaves in America. It tells of hard times, poor living conditions and domestic difficulties. Sometimes it may be humorous but mostly it expresses depression.

The development of Blues to Rock is the story of modern music. Any discussion of where Blues stops and Country, Folk or Rock begin must take into account that the styles of music have overlapped and the differences have been blurred. But the Blues is the basis of all the rhythms of modern popular music.

To examine the rhythm of the Blues … in its simplest form a chord is sounded on the first beat, leaving it to sound, and then it is played again on the second beat, either cutting it off or softening it. This creates a pattern. The process is repeated. It is usually played on a guitar.

Question 1

(a) Why is the Blues important in the history of popular music? [*5 marks*]

(b) What are the main themes of Blues music? [*5 marks*]

(c) Where would you expect to find a passage like this? Give reasons for your answer. [*2 marks*]

PRACTICE QUESTION

Look carefully at the leaflet *Clayton Castle* and answer the following questions:

(a) What three types of information does it provide for the public? List them. [*6 marks*]
(b) How is the leaflet set out to make it easy to read? [*4 marks*]
(c) Find two different styles of writing in the leaflet. Choose examples to support your choice. [*10 marks*]

Discover the sights and sounds of

CLAYTON CASTLE

Travel back over six hundred years and experience the vivid recreation of the sounds and sights of medieval castle life.

Look out for the ghostly Black Duke on the back stairs as he clatters down in full armour, ready to do battle. Listen to the cries and shouts from the stables as the horses are exercised. Peep into the parlour and imagine the ladies at their tapestry work, listening to the sweet sounds of the harp. Explore the kitchens with their massive ovens and spits, where meals for up to a hundred were prepared.

Explore six centuries of dramatic history with a personal audio tour, then watch the video telling the story of this famous fortress.

Clayton Castle was built in the thirteenth century by Edward I as a fortress with typical architectural features: revetment towers, arrow slits and a deep moat for defence. The dungeon has walls ten feet thick.

The castle, built between 1369 and 1388, has an unusual plan of circular towers on either side of a rectangular central block. It has many massive carved beams. Partly rebuilt in Tudor times, the stonework for the façade is in fine condition. Some original Tudor wall paintings were uncovered during recent renovations. The castle has a fine banqueting hall and royal chapel. Each of the massive reception rooms has rich Flemish tapestries and wall-hangings.

Beyond the green lawns around the moat the front drive sweeps through wooded parkland down to the lake, the natural habitat for waterfowl, mandarin and eider ducks, black swans and Russian geese.

CLAYTON CASTLE, Burdenstone, Surrey
01470 713254

Open	**April–Sept.**	**10.00–18.00**
	Oct.–Apr.	**10.00–16.00**
	Closed Sundays, Christmas Day and Boxing Day	
Admission	**Adults**	**£4.00**
	Children	**£2.00**
	Senior Citizens	**£2.50**
	(reductions for groups of ten or more)	
Parking	**Car park to the rear of the castle**	
Other facilities	**Toilets, café, gift shop**	

Reading comprehension: media texts

✓ REVISION TIPS

You probably have the opportunity to see newspapers and magazines every day. When you read them, notice especially how large a part visual display plays in getting the information across. Think, too, about what the writers in the media, or presenters on television information programmes, choose to emphasise as most important. Is it the same as in literature or faction writing? You will find answers to these questions below, in **Topic outline**.

◎ TOPIC OUTLINE

This is the **AT** that you should work towards when reading media material for comprehension:

▶ You should show that you appreciate the way that non-literary media texts are written and that you can weigh up their effectiveness for a reader (**AT2.3**)

The most striking aspect of media texts is their layout. Typically, a newspaper article will have varieties of size and style of print. Most texts of this type have:

▶ a main headline
▶ sub-headlines
▶ bridging capitals
▶ large print for the first paragraph
▶ smaller print for later paragraphs
▶ pictures with captions

The organisation of the text will also be different. The most important part of the message comes first, with lesser details following.

The style may be relaxed, casual and chatty with gossipy details to interest the reader. A fairly straightforward vocabulary may be used with short sentences.

Some literary effects may also occur. The most usual of these are:

▶ exaggeration
▶ comparisons
▶ puns
▶ rhetorical questions
▶ sound patterning of phrases

★ REVISION ACTIVITY

Read the article in Figure 5 from a local newspaper and answer these questions.

Inferior sunglasses will ruin your eyes

Figure 5
Source: Streatham, Clapham, Dulwich Guardian, 10 October 1996

Buyers of sunglasses should be on the lookout for shady deals and bad eyes, trading standards officers have warned.

A survey of sunglasses on sale in Southwark borough found that half did not comply with British safety standards. One third were incorrectly labelled and 17 per cent failed to meet the requirements for protection from harmful ultraviolet rays.

Southwark trading standards officer Hedley Setahul said: 'It is the cheaper sunglasses costing as little as £1 that failed to meet the standards.

'These sunglasses without labelling information on the UV protection they provide are only suitable for cosmetic purposes,' he told the Guardian.

Sunglasses must be tested to a British standard by law, and marked with their UV shade number and a CE mark showing they should have been tested to the standard, setting out the grades of UV shade numbers.

'Wearing poor quality sunglasses can actually cause more damage to the eye than not wearing any,' Mr Setahul said.

'Because of the darkness from the lens, the pupil dilates and takes in more rays from the sun. Wearing sunglasses which don't protect against the sun's ultra violet rays risks causing irreversible eye damage.'

Questions

(a) How is the article made appealing to the reader? You may wish to consider the following in your answer:
  ▶ the layout
  ▶ the order in which information is given
  ▶ any other detail you think important

(b) How does the writer use words to interest the reader? Use examples from the article to support what you say.

PRACTICE QUESTIONS

Look closely at newspaper articles A and B in Figure 6 and answer these questions:

(a) From Article A, list three worrying findings about food in secondary-school canteens. [*6 marks*]

(b) In Article B, what arguments are put forward by the Education Boards to defend the School Meals Service? How convincing are these arguments? [*20 marks*]

(c) How successful is Article A in highlighting the dangers of unhealthy eating? In your answer you should refer to:
  ▶ the picture
  ▶ the headlines
  ▶ the words and phrases used
  ▶ the facts presented
  ▶ anything else you feel is important [*24 marks*] (**NICCEA**)

Article A

Diet 'timebomb' fear ■ School dinners still not making the grade

Figure 6
Source:
Belfast Telegraph

By David Watson
Education Correspondent

ULSTER schoolchildren are still eating too many chips with fatty food 'far in excess' of what the Government recommends as healthy. A critical report carried out for the Northern Ireland Chest, Heart and Stroke Association warned that more must be done to tackle the 'dietary timebomb' which Northern Ireland schoolchildren are 'sitting on'.

The Health Promotion Agency welcomed the report, saying it underlined the fact that children were not eating in a way that would help them prevent later health problems.

Researchers said: 'If successful action is taken, Northern Ireland would be better placed to move down the gloomy international league table of death from heart disease.'

Popular

The report was based on findings from 17 secondary schools.

The team discovered:
• chips are 12 times more popular than baked potatoes
• cakes and biscuits are six times more in demand than fresh fruit

• 46% of calories came from fat, well above the 35% maximum recommended by the Government.

Latest figures, for January 1994, show that 54.5% of pupils take school meals. This amounts to 162,078 pupils from the province's total of 297,433 attending school.

The researchers said the 'most worrying finding' was that 46% of all the calories came from fat.

This was far in excess of the Government's view that the upper level here should be 35%.

This situation alone greatly increases the risk of heart disease in later life.

It was also found that most school meals did not normally provide enough iron or calcium. Many did not have enough vitamin C.

Research

A move away from the cafeteria-style school meals service was urged.

A spokesperson for the research team said: 'We had hoped that this research would identify examples of good practice and encourage all schools to adopt it.

'Sadly, and despite the energetic efforts of many people and organisations, the research has found little good practice to spread.'

But a promising sign in his team's findings was that caterers, teachers and pupils wanted to improve the school meal's healthiness.

Andrew Dougal, NICHA's executive director, said there was concern that the Department of Education guidelines 'may permit excessive quantities of fat' in the meals.

Healthy Options?

Young people know what is good for them and they know what they like . . .

Sarah from Antrim said: 'I love chips and hamburgers. I don't think too much about what I'm eating although my older sister says I should eat more salads.'

John, a student from Belfast, felt there should be 'more choice for vegetarians'.

School Principal, Mr Dunn, said: 'The lessons of healthy eating really begin at home. If they have chips there, they usually choose chips at school.'

Louise McCann:
Enjoying her baked potato and coleslaw

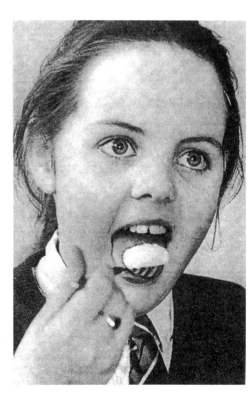

Article B

Attack on school meals 'heartless'

Figure 6 (cont.)
Source:
Belfast Telegraph

By David Watson

THE Northern Ireland Chest, Heart and Stroke Association was today accused of 'kicking school catering in the teeth'.

Education Boards reacted strongly to its report, which claimed that school meals were not healthy enough.

The North-Eastern Education Board said: 'This latest attack is as heartless as the previous outbursts against the quality of school canteen food. It simply isn't justified.'

It said the researchers had ignored primary schools, even though nutrition standards were laid down there by the Government and strictly followed – and had described those in secondary schools as being of poor quality or unhealthy.

Salads

'Such claims are totally unfounded,' said a board spokesman.

The Southern Eastern Education Board said the report did little to commend the present health promoting activities of the meals service.

In its area, 27 of the 34 post-primary schools were members of the Healthy Eating Circle. Salad bars were popular in many schools, showing commitment by staff.

'The pricing policy of menu items is aimed to encourage the uptake of healthy options,' said the spokesman.

He pointed out that many schools had set up their own meals committees. 'These committees provide a check on the healthy choices available.'

He also stressed that his board provided training for its catering staff in promoting healthy eating.

He concluded by saying that Education Boards could only encourage healthy eating but could not insist on it. 'Society today is very much geared to the consumption of fast foods.' he said.

6 Writing: functional

In the exam you need to be able to write in a variety of different ways. The **ATs** which apply to functional writing are that you should be able to:

▶ make use of different forms of writing, including letters, newspaper articles and reviews to suit a range of purposes and contexts (**AT3.1**)
▶ choose a vocabulary which is suited to its purpose and reader and use correct grammar and standard English where appropriate (**AT3.3**)
▶ correct, edit and revise your own writing (**AT3.4**)

There are **six** main types of functional writing that you need to know about for GCSE English:

▶ **Diary**
▶ **Directed summary**
▶ **Letter**
▶ **Newspaper article**
▶ **Report**
▶ **Speech**

Each will be discussed in turn.

Diary

✓ REVISION TIPS

Look out for daily records such as personal diaries, homework diaries, logs, astrology columns in the newspapers. Familiarise yourself with how they are set out and with the styles of writing.

● TOPIC OUTLINE

A diary is a daily record, usually with a fairly brief entry under the day's date, although personal diaries can be much longer. Style can vary from very abbreviated, as in a record of scientific experiments, to chatty in personal entries. The latter have the advantage of giving an opportunity to reflect on matters about which it is not very easy to communicate, face to face. Compare these two examples of genuine diary entries:

19 and 20 April 1681
The weather grew extremely hot beyond the memory of man and so continued hot till 2nd May, Monday, on which day it became cooler, yet no rain.

2 May 1681
Scarce as much rain as would lay the dust.

2 June 1681
Rained at four in the afternoon for an hour or thereabouts, and a little on the 5th and 6th

and so it continues, showing that we were obsessed by the weather even 300 years ago!

> *10 March 1853*
> As we turned the corner of a lane during our walk today a man and a bull came in sight, the former crying out, 'Ladies, save yourselves as well as you can!' the latter scudding onwards slowly but furiously. I jumped aside on a little hedge, but thought the depth below rather too great – about nine or ten feet; but the man cried 'Jump!' and I jumped. To the horror of all, the bull jumped after me . . . I longed to peep at the bull, but was afraid to venture on such a movement. Then I thought, 'I shall probably be killed in a few minutes, how is it that I am not taking it more solemnly. . .'

As in these examples, you will be expected to write in complete sentences, even if the tone of your entry is relaxed. Also remember to give each entry a side heading.

REVISION ACTIVITY

Try keeping your own personal diary for a few weeks.

PRACTICE QUESTION

Write three entries from a teacher's diary. (**London Examinations**)

Directed summary

REVISION TIPS

Directed summary is not a difficult thing to do, but you can underestimate what is involved.

The things to practise and bear in mind are:

▶ Always read the material that you are summarising slowly and carefully first, taking time to understand it.
▶ Work in rough when you are choosing the points you think are important.
▶ Take into account the kind of person who would be likely to read the piece.
▶ Always write in your own words unless there are expressions that are difficult to change.
▶ Do not make the summary too long.

TOPIC OUTLINE

Directed summary involves reading material and picking out certain arguments to convey to another reader. This results in a shorter account than the original, and the emphasis and style will vary, depending on what type of reader is involved. For example, you would convey information about a scheme set up by a supermarket chain to fund computing equipment in local schools differently for the head teachers and the pupils.

The first would want to know how the sponsorship was to be organised and competed for, what sums of money would be involved that might benefit the school or whether there would be donations of actual equipment made directly, whether there was a time limit to the scheme and how a school should go about making an application to take part in the scheme.

The pupils, on the other hand, would want to know what part they could play in sponsored runs, walks and swims, making collections or in some other ways competing for what was being given to schools, and what increased opportunities they would have when the new equipment arrived.

When writing a directed summary you should:

- ▶ read the material you are given steadily to get a general impression of it
- ▶ read the instructions telling you what kind of arguments you need to select
- ▶ read the material again, slowly and carefully, picking out all the points that are relevant to the task set
- ▶ weigh up the relative importance of the ideas you find
- ▶ write them down in the most suitable order to bring out the importance you attach to them, taking care to use your own words as far as possible
- ▶ look again at what type of reader is involved and choose the right style
- ▶ look for instructions about layout, such as a letter or a report form, and follow them
- ▶ write the whole thing out as a draft version
- ▶ check the number of words used and cut out the excess
- ▶ check for any grammar, spelling or punctuation errors
- ▶ write up the final version

A final piece of advice: *do not exceed the word limit*. Remember that examiners count the number of words in summaries and simply cross through all the excess. So don't waste valuable time writing at great length, thinking that the extra will not be noticed.

REVISION ACTIVITY

You can practise these skills for yourself by looking out for articles of interest in the local paper. Choose something that is not too long – about 250 to 300 words – and involves a controversial issue such as cutting down trees in your area, closing a local youth centre or sub-post office. Think of the people who will be especially affected by it, then write a letter to the editor, setting out the arguments on behalf of one group: people who care deeply about the natural environment, or young people who use the youth club, or elderly people who cannot travel far to get their pensions. You may even post the letter and do some good for the community at the same time as you are getting some practice in directed summary.

PRACTICE QUESTION

Imagine that you have been asked to contribute to an *Encyclopaedia of the Cinema*. Read the following passage and write on two topics: first outline what early movie pictures were like, and second describe Charlie Chaplin's skills as a star. Your article should not be more than 150 words.

Charlie Chaplin had tremendous power over people's feelings. Most who saw his film *The Gold Rush* remember how they laughed and cried at the scene where the hungry hero cooks and eats his boot.

His great days as an entertainer were in the early years of the twentieth century when the numbers of people moving to towns to work often long, monotonous hours every day was growing.

They liked nothing better in their leisure hours than to go to the new silent motion picture houses and enjoy the show. This appealed in every country at a time when language was not an issue in cinema. In America, too, where people from many nations had come to live and work, the silent movies provided a common bond.

At first the film studios where Chaplin and his fellow stars worked were rough huts and Hollywood not even a town. Films were turned out quickly to make money and people, used to concerts or theatre, thought them low entertainment. In fact, Chaplin came from the popular theatre himself, and had learned there his skills of miming and comic business. His brilliant characterisation of the little tramp became his trademark.

Feeling limited and powerless as an actor, at first with little status, Chaplin moved into the film business on a wider scale, becoming producer, director, editor and even screenwriter. His early films had no script or plot – they came into being on the spur of the moment. Gradually the whole industry became sophisticated. Chaplin even wrote film music for his later films, most notably the theme of *Limelight*.

His amazing career spanned many years and his contribution to the film industry then and now cannot be praised too highly.

Letter

 REVISION TIPS

This is a form of writing with which you will be very familiar. Make sure that you know the different ways of setting out a letter and expressing its content, depending on the person you are addressing and the purpose of the letter.

 **TOPIC OUTLINE**

The layout, opening, conclusion and general style of a letter should differ depending on the degree of informality or formality involved. Here are the **three main types of letter** you should know:

1 Letter to a friend

---

6 Castle Street
Monday evening

Dear Jo,
I just had to let you know how I got on at the interview. Would have called you, but my phone is out of order.

You'll never guess . . . I GOT THE JOB!

I was really nervous on the way there, but once Mr Jarvis started to talk to me I settled down. It went really well.

See you at the club on Friday and I'll tell you the rest.

Bye,
Janey

2 Letter to someone you know slightly/have heard about but do not know well

> 6 Castle Street
> Broadstairs
> Kent CT13 8UL
> 6 October 1997
>
> Dear Mr Thomas,
> I expect you remember when I worked part-time in the shop last year. I really enjoyed it and would have liked to stay on, but I had to finish my GCSE course.
> I have left school now and am looking for a job. I know that you have no vacancies. I wonder, though, if you would be so kind as to write a reference for me and send it to me by Friday week. I have managed to get an interview, and the manager of the store has asked me to provide a reference from someone who knows about my work outside school.
> I hope that all is going well in the shop. Give my best wishes to Mrs Segal and the staff.
>
> > Yours sincerely,
> > Jane Jonas

3 Letter to someone you do not know/has higher status

> The Manager   6 Castle Street
> Lipman's Fashions Ltd   Broadstairs
> Dover   Kent CT13 8UL
> Kent CT8 5QZ
>   1 October 1998
>
> Dear Sir,
> I am writing in response to the advertisement I saw in the Kent Gazette yesterday for a trainee manageress at your Broadstairs store.
> I left school in July and have passed five subjects in GCSE. I enclose a copy of my results.
> I also have some experience of working in a fashion shop. Over the past two years I have worked at weekends and also had work experience in a local shop, Smarts. As well as serving customers, I spent some time helping the manageress with the accounts and other aspects of running the store.
> I really hope to make my future career in fashion merchandising and would appreciate an interview.
>
> > Yours faithfully,
>
>
> > Miss Jane Jonas

 REVISION ACTIVITY

Make a collection of letters at home, put them in a folder and when you have about a dozen or so group them into types. Decide on the degree of formality in each type and look carefully at the openings, conclusions, layouts and styles.

PRACTICE QUESTION

Write Adrian Mole's letter to a Problem Page (**adapted from London Examinations**)

Newspaper article

REVISION TIPS

There are two main types of newspaper: **tabloids** and **broadsheets**.

Tabloid papers have more pictures, more headlines and less printed text than broadsheets. Whichever type of paper you are writing for, however, you need to be familiar with the typical ways in which newspapers of all kinds communicate with their readers.

If your family regularly takes a newspaper or if you study **journalese** in school, take note especially of these typical features and how effective they can be in communicating a message quickly, dramatically and in an interesting way.

TOPIC OUTLINE

Journalese or writing for newspapers has several distinctive features of layout, organisation and style. Here we consider **four different aspects**:

1 **Layout and presentation**
2 **Organisation of content**
3 **Typical sentence structures**
4 **Typical vocabulary**

Layout and presentation

▶ **Banner headlines**   These are bold, large, heavily inked with capital letters. Their purpose is to catch the reader's attention – and to do this they sometimes take up one-third of a page.

QUEEN MAKES APPEAL

▶ **Sub-headlines**   These are to break up text, so that the reader can take it in gradually, in small amounts. They sometimes offer a skeleton information line, too.

> **Mansion House Speech**
>
> **Serve the Needs of the Family**
>
> **Help the Family Worldwide**
>
> **Speech Well-received**

▶ **Bridging capitals**   These draw the reader's eye into the first paragraph of the text and persuade the reader to go on reading.

> I n her Mansion House speech, on Friday night . . .

▶ **Varied fonts and sizes of type**   Again, the purpose is to keep the reader's interest. The early part of the article will be in larger type than the rest. Sometimes three or four different sizes of type will be used in one article.

> # SACKED AFTER A £1,000 'INDECENT PROPOSAL'
>
> **BRIDE-TO-BE NURSE GLORIA JACKSON, 24, WON A CLAIM OF SEXUAL HARASSMENT AGAINST HER BOSS, DR STANLEY WILLIAMS, YESTERDAY.**
>
> Father-of-five Dr Williams, 55, who has been married twice, says he has no money to pay pretty Gloria compensation.

▶ Pictures   Most news stories these days have some kind of illustration.

Organisation

▶ **News stories**, unlike most others in life, tell you the most exciting, dramatic, important details first. The time sequence in news reporting is dictated by the need to be first with the news and to get it to the readers as quickly and as obviously as possible.

▶ **Content** is usually a mixture of some fact and a good deal of opinion. It is not always easy to tell which is which.

▶ **Other information** included is gossipy personal detail about people in the news, historical or background information and updating or **continuity**, when an ongoing situation is being reported daily. All this means that the organisation of content is much more complicated than that of most stories which are told chronologically, or as they actually happened.

▶ The usual shape of a news story is as follows:
  - **abstract**   This summarises at once what has happened and gives the main point of the story. It answers the question **WHAT IS THIS STORY ABOUT?**

- **orientation**   This sets the scene. It deals with the questions **WHY, WHO, WHERE, WHEN, WHAT WAS THE START OF IT ALL?**
- **complication**   This is the central part of the story and answers the question **THEN WHAT HAPPENED?**
- **evaluation**   This tells you the point of the story and justifies its being told **SO WHAT?**
- **resolution**   This ends the story **WHAT FINALLY HAPPENED?**
- **coda**   This often is a final comment that reminds the reader of similar matters or returns the reader to the present. **SO LIFE GOES ON.**

Typical sentence structures

▶ One of the favourite styles of sentence in news articles is one where the descriptive details come first: that is, before the main noun:

Attractive, thirty-five-year-old mother of four, Mrs Mandy Allen said...

▶ If the details do not come first, they are tucked into parentheses (brackets)

Mrs Mandy Allen (attractive, thirty-five-year-old mother of four) said...

These sentences feed readers' interest in the personal lives of other people and this sells newspapers.

▶ Rhetorical questions often feature in newspaper articles. They involve readers in debate: readers answer in their minds, so keep interested in the arguments put forward.

Why was this woman told to leave her job at a moment's notice?

▶ Triple rhetorical questions. This is more emphatic and helps to persuade the reader to share the view of the writer of the article.

Aren't they guilty? Should they get away with this? Will the British people accept it?

▶ Some sentences, especially in headlines, have parts of speech missing, and are written in shortened form, known as ellipsis. This is often true of headlines or sub-headlines.

QUEEN MAKES APPEAL

This is often done deliberately to create a mystery. At a glance, the reader cannot tell what this is about. Is the Queen appealing for greater privacy for members of the royal family? As that is a topic often in the news and of interest to readers it would encourage people to buy the paper. The 'appeal', though, could have been on behalf of world wildlife or world poverty, couldn't it? You cannot tell. Newspapers thrive on this **ambiguity**.

Typical vocabulary

▶ As space is often strictly limited in newspapers, short words, or **monosyllables**, are often used:

pact, bid, truce, dash, tryst, deal, tell, raid, swoop

▶ **Softener adverbs** are used freely, again to persuade:

obviously, certainly, surely, definitely, surprisingly

▶ **Stereotyping words and phrases** also occur:

hippies, young toughs, nutty professors, trendy vicars

Ellen's climbing every mountain

Figure 7
Source: Streatham,
Clapham, Dulwich
Guardian,
10 October 1996

A young Clapham woman is going on a mountaineering spree to raise money for charity this weekend.

Ellen Pugh will climb Snowdon, Scafell Pike and Ben Nevis in under 36 hours on October 12 and 13, as part of a 1,200-strong team raising more than £200,000 for the youth development charity Raleigh International.

The 18-year-old, from Rectory Grove, will then join one of Raleigh's International's 10-week expeditions to a remote part of the world on a community and conservation project.

▶ **Verbal patterning** makes newspaper copy memorable and entertaining:

Three young girls – hungry, homeless and hopeless – bed down on the streets of London.

REVISION ACTIVITY

Figure 7 shows a small news story from a local paper. Read it through, then answer the following questions:

(a) How does the presentation help to get the information across?
(b) Try to work out how the story is organised. Can you find an abstract, orientation and evaluation?
(c) Pick out two sentences and explain how they are typical of newspaper style.

Try doing this for articles you read in local or national newspapers.

PRACTICE QUESTION

Many people feel that there is increasing harassment in the workplace. Write an article for a newspaper about a case of harassment which came to court.

Report

REVISION TIPS

Reports can be quite unfamiliar to many candidates. They are not the sort of thing that students are asked to write for course work; they belong more to the world of work, later in life. However, exam questions do ask for reports every now and again, so it is as well to be prepared to write one.

The best preparation to make is to learn to retell or rewrite something clearly, in formal or at least direct, businesslike English and take care with the order of events. Learn to distinguish between fact and opinion and to formulate your own suggestions as to how a situation may be followed up.

TOPIC OUTLINE

Usually you are given a body of information and then asked to write a report about it. The following are essential for any report:

▶ Find out who the report is written to and at what location. The date can also be significant. Put a clear heading, giving this information at the top of the page.

To the Councillor for Housing, Lambeth
Report on a visit to 321 Gothic Road Wednesday 8 May 1997

▶ Give the facts in a clearly organised group of paragraphs in the best order to make the situation clear.
▶ Offer some recommendations about how the situation should be handled.
▶ Write in a clear, businesslike style – you cannot be too plain.
▶ Finish the report with a formal signature.

REVISION ACTIVITY

Read the information below, and then answer the question that follows.

School age raised to 6

Suggestions have been made occasionally that the age of admission to school should be raised to six, and the infant shortage in some parts of the country may soon make such a course of action necessary.

Staff shortages caused one local education authority to arrange for children becoming five during a term to have half-time education only.

Parents were sent a questionnaire asking them if they thought this had been harmful, beneficial, or made no difference.

All responded. Only 2% thought it had been harmful, 21% were undecided and the rest thought there were some advantages to the scheme.

These comments were made by parents: 'I think having to attend just in the mornings helped her to accept school more easily. It helped her get used to the routine and gave her more self-confidence.' 'He has really enjoyed school from the start and I think this is because of the half-time attendance.' 'Starting school is a big wrench for lots of children. This way, they get used to going away from home for only a couple of hours at first.' 'A long school day is tiring for young children at first. Half-time gets them used to the new pattern.'

Teachers where this new scheme was tried out were also mainly enthusiastic. One of them reported a higher rate of attendance than usual in the Reception Class. Another said that the children were always bright and lively. Half-time education could be a solution to some of the problems of early education. Staffing would be eased and more part-time teachers could be employed. Children would have the security of working with the same teacher.

Imagine that you are a head teacher reporting on this scheme to the Parents' Association. Write two paragraphs from the report, giving

1 the advantages parents found in the scheme
2 the advantages teachers found in the scheme

End with a recommendation about whether the scheme should be adopted by your own school.

PRACTICE QUESTION

1 Read the passage from *Smokestack Lightning* by Laurence Staig on pages 20–21. Laurence's mother has applied for a council flat. A housing officer has to visit the house and write a report on their present accommodation. Write the housing officer's report. (**London Examinations**)

Speech

Writing a speech to be given to an audience, either in favour of the topic involved or arguing against it, may be set in the exam and it is a kind of writing that most students enjoy. However, quite a lot of skill is involved in getting your points across and keeping your listeners interested.

One of the best preparations is to tune in to the many opportunities given by radio and television to listen to the speeches of people you personally find persuasive. Try to work out how they put their arguments together in a compelling way.

TOPIC OUTLINE

The main aim of a speech is to persuade your listeners to agree with your particular point of view. The ability of the speech writer to do this **depends on two things**:

1 **good structure**
2 **persuasive argument**

Here is a useful outline for any speech:

For/against the motion

Statement of the proposition

That this House believes that television, film and video has a bad effect on children's behaviour.

Appeal to common knowledge

We all know that there is more violence and crime in our society...

Personal belief

I believe that this is partly caused by the television, film and video that young people watch...

For example: give an example that all your listeners will know about:

Let me give you an example: a fourteen-year-old girl, who saw a documentary on television about theft from shops by return of so-called damaged goods, went on a spree stealing clothes worth £800.

Give more examples to convince your listeners:

I could give you many more examples...

Consider the arguments for the opposition:

Others will say that television, film and video educates, broadens the minds of young people, but...

Provide some data from an authoritative source:

Professor Broadbent's research at Cambridge University proves...

Urge your listeners to support your proposition:

I urge you to support me and vote for this motion.

Here are some of the effects of style that will help you to persuade your listeners:

Balanced argument:

Television is both educational and entertaining.

Antithesis (opposites):

Television is educational not damaging.

Ladder argument:

Television is educational, it is entertaining – and it is here to stay.

Exaggeration:

Television is the greatest force in our society for moulding the characters of young people.

Persuader adverbs:

Obviously, television is an influence we cannot ignore.

Imagery:

Television provides a torrent of images, pouring into our homes daily.

REVISION ACTIVITY

Listen to the speeches of speakers you admire and take note of the effects of style they use.

PRACTICE QUESTION

Write two speeches, one in favour and one against the motion that it is a good thing to fight for one's country.

Writing: creative

Descriptive writing

Good description depends on the careful use of words. This does not mean using impressive or unusual words, but it does mean trying as hard as you can to describe whatever it is, as clearly and vividly as possible. You may use some images, too, but do this sparingly.

A common error is 'overwriting', or being too elaborate, so that the reader gets a confused impression and sometimes even a ridiculous one. The opposite is writing in cliché, that is using overworked words and phrases. This can take the life away from what you are describing.

Compare:

(a) Her face, drained of its natural colour, seemed tense, with tight-drawn muscles, and her eyes stared without seeing.

(b) Her face went ashen-white, like freshly-driven snow, and seemed as hard as marble, while her eyes were like those of a sleep-walker. (**too many images**)

(c) Her face was as white as a sheet and her eyes stared blankly. (**cliché**)

Remember, too, that descriptive writing needs a good shape: don't let it ramble.

● TOPIC OUTLINE

Many students think they are good at **descriptive writing**. Piling up adjectives and elaborate phrases is not necessarily good description. Some well-chosen adjectives and participles can be effective but overwriting can irritate. Consider the example below which describes getting dressed up to go out on a date. The adjectives and participles are in italics:

> Will jeans be too *casual*? Out come the *faded blue* ones, the *sky-on-a-summer's-day* ones, the *grey-blue* ones and the *midnight blue* ones. I make up my mind that none of them will do. But there are always the *charcoal* ones, the *black* ones, the *white* ones and even the *ripped* ones. Casually throwing them all on to a chair I finally choose the ones with *colourful* patches all over them, and then wonder whether it would be better to wear a skirt. The only question is – which one? Should it be the *pleated* one or the *mini*, the *leather-look* one or the *suede*; the *figure-hugging* one, with the frills at the bottom, or the *wrap-around*? Finally, there is the *baggy* one and the provocatively *sexy* one. With *half* my wardrobe at my feet, I finally settle on the skirt with the *colourful patches* over it.

This is well-controlled and amusing, but imagine the description continuing like this for three or four pages. If you were giving a careful description of action, on the other hand, you might use chiefly verbs and adverbs, as in the next example. The verbs and adverbs are in italics.

The umpire *called* 'Over'. The batsmen *left* ends *to confer* in the middle. The captain *called* a player *over*; as he *tossed* him the ball he *gave* a stern look. He *knew exactly* what *was expected* of him. He *turned* his back and *started walking slowly away*, being careful *to take* equal strides. He *reached* his mark, twenty yards from the wicket. As he *slowly turned*, he *listened carefully* – the crowd *were yelling* with expectation, his team-mates *were clapping out* encouragement. He *placed* the ball in his hand. He *took* a deep breath and *started* his run up, a slow *canter* at first, but *gradually getting faster* and *faster*, *until* he *was* at full speed as he *reached* the crease. He *leaped* into his delivery stride, at the same time *raising* both arms into position and *released* the ball from his hand, *transferring* all his momentum. The ball *struck* the batsman's pads in line with the stumps.

HOWZATT!! He *turned around slowly to see* the umpire *raise* his finger.

You could take some ideas from these examples – but don't overdo it. Both of these examples are of things precisely observed, usually seen but, in the last instance, also heard. They also use the human senses. This kind of description is usually called **literal** – actually there to be sensed in the real world.

There is a different way of describing, though, that is oblique, or **figurative**. Here you compare, usually in an image, what you want to describe with something which has features in common with it. This is an old rhetorical device called, in its simplest form, a **simile**: a comparison introduced by 'like' or 'as':

She chose an outfit that would make her look lithe like a cat.
She sidled into the room as insidiously as a cat.

We use these expressions quite often in everyday speech and so they sometimes get overworked. Such worn-out comparisons are called **clichés**, and are best avoided in writing:

He had a voice like thunder.
She was as cold as ice.

A direct comparison is called a **metaphor**:

He thundered down the stairs.
She gave him an icy stare.

You could occasionally try using an image right through a paragraph or a piece of writing – this is know as **extended metaphor**.

At this time of her life she felt as if she were sitting in the boughs of a tree, heavy with fruit. Above her hung the shining apples. Each apple was something she hoped to attain: a successful career, marriage, children, a house of her own, travelling the world, looking good. She had only to reach out to take one – ah, but which one should she reach for first?

If you are asked to do **free writing**, that is with content of your own choice, you may describe in any way you like. At other times you may be asked to write in a way that is related to a passage set for comprehension. In this case, you should not go far beyond the details of the set passage.

REVISION ACTIVITY

Write a descriptive paragraph, with an opening and concluding phrase, and a central stretch giving as much detail as possible. Concentrate either on using many adjectives or many verbs and adverbs.

PRACTICE QUESTION

Write about a topic of your choice from an unusual point of view.

Dramatic writing

REVISION TIPS

Much of the drama that we see on film and television seems just like life. The action absorbs us, so that we seem to live it ourselves, and the speech of the actors impresses us in much the same way. But both action and speech have been written by script writers who know that dramatic plot is not just life situations recorded on the page, and that dialogue is very different from normal speech.

As you watch plays or read them, look out for the different methods that dramatists and script writers use. Film plots are usually much more complex and sophisticated than those of written drama in the way they are organised. For example, a murder mystery may open with the crime itself, though the villain may be seen only by his hands or, in one memorable example, Spielberg's *Duel*, by his boots.

Dialogue is not easy to analyse from the screen but if you look closely at any plays you are studying in school you will be able to see how it differs from ordinary speech.

A useful revision activity is to write in dialogue (as if for television drama) some conversation that you have heard at home or at school or college. Set out the location, name the main characters and then write down exactly what you can remember them saying. Even better, write it down as the conversation is taking place, or tape it (with their permission). When you read it back, if you have written down verbatim speech, you will be surprised how difficult it is to follow. The advice immediately following will help you to transform rough and ready conversation into streamlined, effective dialogue.

TOPIC OUTLINE

Dramatic plots need at least **three elements**:

1 **Exposition**   This tells us what we need to know to follow the action. It may be where it took place, what sort of people the main characters are, and what the dramatic situation is.
2 **Development**   This shows some kind of complication of the action, maybe conflict between the characters.
3 **Resolution**   This sorts out the situation and often concludes it with a happy or moral ending – or, if not, an ending that satisfies readers, listeners or viewers. Sometimes plays are 'open ended', and leave the fate of the characters to be thought about.

Most dramas have at least **five types of character**:

1 **Protagonist**   This is the main character, who develops, whose situation changes and who is closely involved in the action.
2 **Modifier**   This is the character who brings about the change in the protagonist.
3 **Antagonist**   This is the character who opposes the protagonist (and is sometimes the same as the modifier).

4 Supporting   These are extra characters either on the side of the protagonist or the antagonist.

5 Functional   These are characters such as the postman or the taxi driver who provide a lifelike context for the action.

Finally, there are several differences to remember between **ordinary speech** and **dialogue**. **Dialogue** is:

▶ *Selective*   Remarks are limited to those which make a dramatic point.

▶ *Often in complete sentences*   It has fewer breaks and false starts.

▶ *Pointed*   It is directed to the immediate situation.

▶ *Without non-verbal features*   It lacks gesture and glance.

▶ *Without tone or mood*   These have to be added by the actor.

In comparison, **ordinary speech** is:

▶ *Complex in structure*   There are more broken sentences and long, continuous, rambling stretches.

▶ *Hesitant*   It has many pauses, 'hmns' and 'ers'.

▶ *Full of tone and mood*   It has emphasis, volume and pitch.

▶ *Accompanied by non-verbal features*   Such as glances and gestures.

You will find that **dialogue** is easier to punctuate than **direct speech**, because you can **cut out the inverted commas**:

> [The scene is a corner shop, a newsagent's. A young man comes running along the street, and hurtles into the open doorway, gasping for breath.]
> *Shopkeeper*: (startled) Can I help you?
> *Young man*: (still breathing hard) Well, just a minute, and I'll tell you ...
> *Shopkeeper*: Tell me what?
> *Young man*: What happened, just along the street ...

If this were part of a **dramatic narrative**, you would have to set it out as **conversation**, and it would look like this:

> The street outside the newsagent's was deserted. Suddenly, a young man came running along the street and hurtled into the open doorway, gasping for breath. The shopkeeper was startled and asked, 'Can I help you?'
>   The young man could not speak at first, because he was breathing so hard, but at last he gasped, 'Well, just a minute, and I'll tell you ... '
>   'Tell me what?' asked the shopkeeper.
>   The young man replied, 'What's happened, just now, along the street here ... '

★ ### REVISION ACTIVITY

Read and make a list of critical points about this short scene, written by a sixteen-year-old student.

THE BLACK SHEEP OF THE FAMILY

> (A suburban house, 13 Acacia Avenue. It is 8.30 am. A postcard flutters through the letter box on to the mat.)
> *Dawn*: Mum, there's a card here and it's from someone called Uncle Douglas. He says he's coming to visit. Who's Uncle Douglas?
> *Mum*: Are you sure it says 'Douglas'?
> *Dawn*: Here, see for yourself ...
> (A week later. The doorbell is rung sharply twice. Dawn goes to the door.)
> *Dawn*: Mum – it's Uncle Douglas!
> *Mum*: Oh, God.
> *Dawn*: Mum, are you coming?

Mum: (peering anxiously round the door) Douglas, is it really you? After all these years? Oh, I feel faint. (Sits down on the hall chair. Inside the house a young child starts crying.)

Douglas: (cheerfully) Oh, what a way to treat your long-lost brother. What a greeting, uh!

Dawn: Look, just who are you? You turn up at this house and the next thing I know is Mum has fainted. You had better be genuine, mister.

Douglas: It's me, Sis. It's me, Douglas. Don't you remember your own brother?

Mum: (now standing, leaning on the chair. She looks at him long and hard. Her mouth and eyes soften a little, and then she tenses up) You're not my brother. He left long ago. No, you're not Doug. I don't know you. He left me all alone, with no one to help me; I was left to fend for myself, to pay his debts. I was willing to do it – I loved him then.

Douglas: Sis, Sis, come on. Don't be like this. It is me. I promise I won't leave you again. (awkwardly) The truth is, I'm rather down on my luck just now. Look, if you could just let me have £20, I'll be off.

Mum: How dare you! Just get out!

Dawn: Do as Mum says. Can't you see she's upset? (Inside the child continues crying.)

Douglas: But Sis . . .

Mum: Don't call me Sis. Just leave. (Douglas bows his head and backs out of the door.) Shut that door, Dawn, and lock it.

Dawn: Who was that man and why did he come?

Mum: That was your Uncle Douglas, the black sheep of the family. Take a good look because you won't be seeing him again, for a long time. (Through the window they both watch him walking down the street, Dawn with a confused stare, Mum with tears in her eyes.)

 PRACTICE QUESTION

Interview one of the people in the prereleased book *Places* for a radio programme called 'People and Places'. You may like to set out your answer in the form of a drama script. (**SEG**)

Imaginative writing

 **REVISION TIPS**

At first thought, **imaginative writing** may seem far removed from reality. Some of the best writing of this kind, though, is based on observation from real life. If you think of science-fiction writing, or ghost stories, some of the most frightening effects are not given full detail – the reader is made to build up tension gradually from hints and suggestions – or else some variation in the natural world occurs. Can *you* think of an absolutely new idea?

 **TOPIC OUTLINE**

There are few rules here, as the best imaginative writing is individual. One idea that is worth trying is to think of an image that resembles some situation in the real world, or a human experience – such as War as a game of skill and chance, School as a prison – and develop an essay around it, drawing out all the similarities between the two. Alternatively, take a perfectly ordinary day and have something extraordinary happen.

REVISION ACTIVITY

1 Suppose that, digging in the flower bed at the end of the garden, you suddenly turn up on your spade a patch of earth which is a new colour. It isn't a shade you have ever seen before. You think you have discovered a brand new natural colour. Write a paragraph about the incident and try to describe exactly what you have found.

PRACTICE QUESTION

1 Write about an imagined experience using the title *Nightmare in Daylight*.

Narrative writing

REVISION TIPS

Most candidates enjoy writing narratives and find it easier than some other types of writing. Things can go wrong, though. Good narrative writing has the same control and structure that was just discussed for dramatic plots. Beginnings and endings, too, are important. You need to begin in a way that makes your reader keen to read on, and end in a way that satisfies. One of the worst endings is: 'And then the alarm clock went off and I realised it had all been a dream.' This shows that the writer could not handle the situation developed in the narrative, so just found a way to stop. That is feeble craftsmanship.

Remember that **narrative** and **story**, though closely related, are not exactly the same thing.

▶ **Narrative** is, strictly speaking, retelling events which are chronologically arranged.

> I was driving along the High Street when I saw two men wearing anoraks waiting outside a post-office. One of them went inside. Soon afterwards he came out, carrying something. The two men got into a nearby car and drove away at speed. I called the police on a mobile phone and gave them the car number.

▶ **Story** has a theme, a situation and a complication. Usually, if we are involved, we tend to give ourselves heroic status and embroider some of the plain facts, when we tell or write about them.

> As I was driving along the High Street I was worrying about the rising crime rate in my neighbourhood, reported in the local paper. What was happening to this sleepy country area? Was this what I had moved from the city for? Suddenly, I saw two sinister-looking men, their faces concealed in the hoods of their anoraks, hanging about outside the post-office. Immediately I had my suspicions when I saw one go in while the other waited outside, presumably with the get-away car. Brushing aside thoughts of danger, I drove across and parked behind the robbers' vehicle. When I saw one of the villains come out carrying what looked like a bag and jump into the get-away vehicle, I grabbed my mobile phone and gave their number to the police. What a story I would have to tell when I got to work later that morning!

You see the difference. The first is just facts, simply told and plainly arranged, as the events took place. The second is facts plus interpretation, with glimpses of the narrator's thoughts and feelings. It has a prevailing theme. The truth of the matter could well be that the two men were window-cleaners on a cold morning, just doing their work – but stories are to entertain, not to deal with the facts alone.

Collect ideas for writing from other people's stories. Notice good endings, interesting turns of plot and vivid ways of describing character. Read as many stories as you can.

TOPIC OUTLINE

All stories have **certain characteristics**. These are:

► *A good opening*   Make your reader want to read on. You may begin at the beginning but you could experiment. Plunge straight into the story at the point when something exciting or important is about to happen, or begin looking back, knowing all the events, and starting to retell them retrospectively.

► *Selection of events*   Choose events which bring out the theme or tell the reader more about the characters. In dramatic stories plant early clues about the development and build up to a climax.

► *Satisfying endings*   These may be the final action but you could state your theme, point to a moral, or be 'open-ended', leaving the reader to decide the outcome.

► *A point of view*   This may be the narrator's or it may be that of one of the characters.

► *A suitable style*   This will depend on whether the story is told by a narrator, who is distanced from the events, or a character directly involved in and affected by them. Consider how your style would need to differ if you told the outline 'robbery' story above first from the viewpoint of one of the waiting men and, second, from that of the policeman called upon to investigate the crime.

In GCSE examinations **three types of story writing** are mainly involved:

1 **Dramatic narrative**   This must catch and hold the attention of the reader from the start. To first obtain and then sustain this level of impact you must select your incidents carefully, pace the action so that it moves swiftly along or slows to an almost unbearable tension in parts, then races to the dreadful climax. Your characters must be essential to the action. Your style can be plain, direct, terse, maybe with snatches of dialogue and some atmospheric description.

2 **Story continuation**   Here you are given a start and asked to develop it. You must keep to the style of the original and develop the characters you are given, perhaps with one or two more, but don't add too many or your story will become cluttered and your characters shadowy. Avoid a distinction between the start and your own continuation – there should be no 'join'. Above all, *be relevant*. Don't be tempted to use the start as a 'jumping off' point and continue with something completely different.

3 **'Open' narrative**   Here you are just given a title to write about as you wish. In fact, it is much less easy for a reader to predict how the story will develop, so you need to work hard at your opening. **Irrelevance** can also be a problem here, if you misapply the title. Think of a story that fits the title and jot down an outline plan, to make sure you don't wander off the point.

REVISION ACTIVITY

1 Find a short, plain account, perhaps in a local paper, of some action. Rewrite it as a story, bring out its potential for complication, adding mood and developing some of the characters involved.

2 Write a short story where two people are locked in conflict, first from the point of view of one of them, then the other – for example, a difference of opinion between a parent and a teenage child.

PRACTICE QUESTION

Write a thriller from the viewpoint of a third-person narrator while the action is taking place.

Personal writing

REVISION TIPS

This is a good choice of writing for most people. You can write vividly about experiences that have been really important to you. Remember, though, that an experience that seems very obvious to you, because you have lived through it, may need to be made clear to the reader.

A common error is to forget to sustain the first-person narrator: to begin: 'I remember the night of the party very well,' but continue 'Philip remembered the look on his mother's face.' Sometimes, it is the other way round – a student may begin writing about 'Philip', then lapse into the first person.

Another error is to fail to give the piece of work any shape. It is tempting to write at great length about personal experiences, telling it just as it was, but it is often better to think the work out first, and present a satisfying arrangement of incident with some later reflection.

TOPIC OUTLINE

Spend some time thinking over and around what you have chosen to write about. Consider different ways of presenting it: you could start at the end, and recap earlier events, or you could be very selective and just pick out vivid and memorable details.

Whatever you choose to do, keep as close to the experience as you can.

REVISION ACTIVITY

Write about a moment in the past of great significance to you.

PRACTICE QUESTION

The following poem was set as part of prereleased material for forthcoming exams. Read it once or twice and then write about your memories of early school days. (**London Examinations**)

Half-past Two

Once upon a schooltime
He did Something Very Wrong
(I forget what it was).

And She said he'd done
Something Very Wrong, and must
Stay in the school-room, till half-past two.

(Being cross, she'd forgotten
She hadn't taught him Time.
He was too scared of being wicked to remind her.)

He knew a lot of time: he knew
Gettinguptime, timeyouwereofftime,
Timetogohomenowtime, TVtime,

Timeformykisstime (that was Grantime).
All the important times he knew,
But not half-past two.

He knew the clockface, the little eyes
And two long legs for walking,
But he couldn't click its language.

So he waited, beyond onceuponatime
Out of reach of all the timefors,
And knew he'd escaped for ever

Into the smell of old chrysanthemums on Her desk,
Into the silent noise his hangnail made,
Into the air outside the window, into ever.

And then 'My goodness,' she said,
Scuttling in, 'I forgot all about you.
Run along or you'll be late.'

So she slotted him back into schooltime,
And he got home in time for teatime,
Nexttime, notimeforthatnowtime,

But he never forgot how once by not knowing time,
He escaped into the lockless land of ever,
Where time hides tick-less waiting to be born.

U.A. Fanthorpe

Persuasive writing

REVISION TIPS

We all spend a good deal of our time exchanging views and trying to persuade others to share our own. All around us we are open to the persuasive arguments of others, as in selling methods, for example. Believing in the idea or product, though, is not always enough. We have to find the best way of expressing our ideas to make others believe us.

Take notice of commercials that attract you. How do they create their effects? If you listen to a live interview, or a studio discussion, notice which speakers seem to get most attention and use some of their methods yourself.

TOPIC OUTLINE

There are **four golden rules** for effective persuasive argument:

1 **Get your facts right**
2 **Take account of the opposing viewpoint**
3 **Plan and structure your argument well**
4 **Aim to hold the reader's attention**

Arguments can be presented for both sides of an issue – this is called giving **a balanced view**. This type of argument is difficult if you personally feel strongly about the issue. It is fairest, perhaps, as it enables readers to see all round an issue and to make up their own minds. Alternatively, one point of view may be urged, and another ignored, suppressed or distorted. How can that be fair? Well, some consider that the end justifies the means. We see this happening in advertising, politics, in any situation where the person, trying to persuade us to accept a point of view, feels that it is important to do so. This is **persuasive argument**.

Don't confuse **argument** with **assertion**. **Argument** involves giving reasons to support your views; **assertion** means just saying that something is so, without giving any evidence to support the view at all:

> *Angela*: The money raised by the sponsored school run is going to be spent on a minibus.
>
> *Babs*: How do you know that? Don't you mean it will go into a fund towards buying a minibus, because we didn't raise that much money, did we?
>
> *Angela*: Everyone says we'll have a new bus. Anyway, what I said is the same as what you've just said.
>
> *Babs*: No, it isn't. First, what do you mean by 'everyone'? How many people have told you? Oh, and another thing, I happen to have seen the list of donations and the total was £250. That wouldn't buy a decent motor bike, let alone a minibus.
>
> *Angela*: Oh, you always do argue so!

Babs has certainly got the better of this discussion, because Angela is only putting forward assertions, whereas Babs first questions her friend's opinion, wanting to know more about it; next she puts forward her own proposed modification of her friend's assertion, giving a reason, which turns Babs' remarks into argument. So Babs wins the exchange but she lacks the powers of persuasion. Angela feels defeated and bad-tempered. It is better, if you can, to win the argument gracefully, leaving your opponent well-disposed towards you.

1 **Get your facts right**
   It is always worth while 'doing your homework' about any issue you are putting forward, otherwise your readers can prove you wrong. If you are well-informed you are in control.

2 **Take account of the opposing viewpoint**
   An argument is always more persuasive if you have anticipated the objections that may be raised against it and have answers to them. 'I know you think that . . . but I hope to show you that there is a better view'; 'You may have read that . . . but that is not all you need to know' and so on.

3 **Plan and structure your argument well**
   Spend time thinking especially about your **opening**, arranging your ideas from the most to the least important, linking the main branches of argument and your conclusion.

Openings matter, because this is how you will first catch your reader's interest. You could use any of the following methods and you can probably think of others for yourself:

(a) an attention-catching statement
(b) a small narrative example
(c) a significant statistic
(d) a personal appeal to the reader
(e) a quotation
(f) your main proposition

Compare the following openings of two persuasive essays. Which makes you want to read on, and why? Which of the above six opening strategies are used by each writer?

> **A** 'Cruelty out of vanity' – that is what I think of when people talk about cosmetics. Why do we need to enhance our own natural features to appear more beautiful for the modern world? Wrinkle creams, moisturisers, toners, cleansers – we say we need them all! It seems that humans will never be satisfied with what they already have.

> **B** Once again, the examinations are behind me. My holidays are here once again and it is time to learn – not from books, but from travel – that word which carries with it fascinating things, sometimes even beyond imagination, and frustration, too, that can turn me crazy. It is time to leave home on a visit to a new land.

They are both attention-catching. Did you notice that the first begins with openings (a), (d) and (e) above? First there is the quotation, then the rhetorical question, appealing directly to the reader's conscience. The paragraph ends with a strong declaration of viewpoint. The second looks like (b): the writer is starting to tell us about the personal experience of travel – its pleasures, lessons and frustrations – before launching into a full discussion of its merits and demerits.

Organising arguments

The best way to see which are the major and which the minor ideas and examples is to draw a topic tree (see page 23). Then you can see at a glance how best to bring out the main ideas, the lesser points and the examples.

Linking arguments

You need to make clear links between your points to help your reader to follow your case. You could jot down a set of headings such as:

(a) This discussion is about . . .
(b) Some people think . . . ; there is some evidence that . . .
(c) But I disagree . . . ; giving contrary evidence that . . .
(d) You yourself may have heard and believe that . . .
(e) However, I am offering evidence to persuade you that . . .
(f) I hope you will agree with me that . . . is the right view.

Conclusions

Sometimes students are so glad to have reached the end of a piece of work that they just stop and put down the biro. You can almost hear the sigh of relief! On the other hand, sometimes a student will repeat in summary all the main points with none of the subtleties of argument given earlier, so providing a boring and repetitive conclusion. Don't do either of these. Instead do one of the following:

(a) Restate your opening, but more emphatically.
(b) Review your opening, showing how it can now be seen differently.
(c) Choose a good quotation to sum up your case.

(d) Give your personal evaluation.

(e) Leave the ending open, but suggest a way ahead.

(f) Invite the reader to share your concluding idea, or else think of a way ahead.

Here are the conclusions to essays **A** and **B** above; you read their openings, remember. Again try to match them to the six types suggested in the list above:

> **A** I disagree with the companies who claim that it [the use of cosmetics] is necessary, and that people will benefit from it. After all, who wears the cosmetics and uses the toiletries? Do we – or the animals?

> **B** To sum up: travel, whether pleasant or frustrating, is a rewarding experience. Let travel be via any mode of transport – land, air or sea: it is one of the greatest pleasures in life.

Both of these are successful, aren't they? **A** uses (d) and (f), challenging the reader to disagree; **B** uses (b) and (d), ending emphatically with a personal judgement.

Aim to hold the reader's attention

The best way to do this is to pay attention to **style**. Here are some examples of devices used by writers **A** and **B** above.

▶ **Conflation**   Here two ideas, which aren't necessarily connected, are linked, to look as if they are similar:

> It is time once again to learn, not from books but from travel.

▶ **Exaggeration**   Here the case is overstated:

> You may agree with the writer that 'travel is one of the greatest pleasures in life', but would you feel the same if he or she had written 'Travel is the only pleasure in life'?

▶ **Generalisation**   This broad statement is helpful in putting a case, but too many will make your writing seem vague. In both the following examples we feel the persuasion, but may tend to differ to some extent.

> Travel ... is a rewarding experience;
> travel ... is one of the greatest pleasures in life.

▶ **Persuader words**   These words (usually adverbs) or phrases have no function beyond urging the reader to agree:

> After all ... who wears the cosmetics?

▶ **Repetition**   You can hammer home your point by repeating, but don't do it *too* often, or you will try the patience of your reader!

> Once again the examinations are behind me ... once again it is time to learn

▶ **Rhetorical question**   This type of question needs no immediate answer, but is addressed to the reader directly:

> After all, *who wears the cosmetics and uses the toiletries? Do we – or the animals?*

REVISION ACTIVITY

Read the complete text of **A**'s essay then pick out as many of the above devices of style as you can.

What are your opinions on cosmetics and toiletries?

'Cruelty out of vanity' – that is what I think of when people talk about cosmetics. Why do we need to enhance our own natural features to appear more beautiful for the modern world? Wrinkle creams, moisturisers, toners, cleansers – we say we need them all! It seems that humans will never be satisfied with what they already have.

The issue of 'beauty kills' is one to which I feel I can relate. I, myself, do not believe in procedures such as eye-irritancy tests, just to see if a product is worth-while. Animals suffer every day for the hungry public, anxious to better themselves more and more, outdoing one another. And yet, do they stop to consider the vicious barbarity of it all? Take, for example, a normal, healthy young rabbit. Think about the freedom that you yourself have, and try to realise what it would be like to have it ripped away from you. This is how we can relate to the rabbit.

Imagine the bitter struggle of trying to move in a cramped cage, desperately, but hopelessly, clawing your way through the cold metal bars. The want and need to get out is overpowering, but strength is not enough. Then, suddenly, your hopes are lifted; the cage is opened, and you are handled by warm, smooth hands. As you are placed on to a sleek, shiny table, you look around and see hundreds of other cages lined up, each and every one of them occupied by an animal, probably with similar hopes of escape. The rest of the room is white and bright. There are lots of instruments and technical things.

The person who took you out of the cage advances towards you with something in his hands. It's small but shiny. You get a quick glimpse of the object but, without warning, you feel a sharp blow from behind. Your eyes widen with terror; you give a piercing scream of pain. You begin to claw at the table, struggling to break free. A quick movement from behind pulls you back, holding and pinning you down – a crushing blow. You feel weak and tired. You have no energy. Your reserves have diminished in one quick moment. Your body shifts its weight and flops. There is no movement. Your body is still and quiet.

In the modern world in which we live today, I find it very distressing that we continue to treat the animal population with methods that torture.

They have just as much right to life and freedom as we do. Why can't advances in technology do anything to prevent these cases? If some shops and brand names refuse to use cruelty as part of their products, why on earth can't others?

I disagree with the companies who claim that it is necessary, and that people will benefit from it. After all, who wears the cosmetics and uses the toiletries? Do we – or the animals?

PRACTICE QUESTION

Write in support of an issue that you feel strongly about concerning the rights of children.

8 Spelling, handwriting and presentation

Ten per cent of your marks for Writing are allocated to spelling, handwriting and presentation.

According to **AT4/5** candidates must demonstrate in their writing that they can:

► spell common words
► write legibly and present finished work clearly and attractively

Tips for improving these skills were given in Part I (pages 2 and 6). Also note that punctuation is assessed as part of the writing grade, not separately.

Here is an exercise which will give you some idea of the standard required for a weak grade and a good grade.

 PRACTICE QUESTION

Read the three samples from answers written during an exam and suggest how many marks out of ten each should be awarded. (Assume that the handwriting in each is legible.)

1   There are a lot of things that can be recycled such as Paper, glass, metal, organic waste, Dead flowrs, Potato Peelings and tea leaves. I think that all of this is a very good idear, as it would be a nicer Place to live in. It also cuts down the amount of enrgy needed to make that item. less heat means using less oil or coal. Recycled rubish do's not cost anything to Recyele so i think that more People should Do this all it involve is going down to your nerist reccycleing Bank and Put what you have got to recycle in to the aprort skip. So i think recycling is a very good ider.

2   Pick up any litter or rubish and put it in a bag. Take it to a sorting base where they can unmix it and then send it off to be recycled. Sounds easy enough, you thought someone would already be doing it. Well they probably arn't so do your bit, just spend a hour or so picking up rubbish in your street or your local park.
    Another way to stop the litter build up is to write to your local council and complain about the mess and how unsafe the rubish is and ask what the intend to do about it. You could even ask or demand road sweepers to do the job.

3   Recycling is a very good idea. If we didn't have the equipment to recycle, Britain (and indeed the world) would be a very polluted and unpleasant place. I don't think there would be any life, in fact. Bearing this in mind, I'm surprised recycling is not compulsory. Recycling has such a good, simple effect. Energy is saved obviously; materials are also saved and also you save time as well, because you don't need to bother about finding substitute materials to make the same item. Rubbish that we throw away is taken to be dumped in huge landfill sites. Although most sites eventually get covered with soil, they cannot be used to grow crops, and they are not compacted enough for building.

Answers
Speaking and listening: the individual oral

STUDENT'S RESPONSES AND GRADING: PRACTICE QUESTIONS TOPICS 1–4

Question 1
Give your views on advertisements which shock.

Student A
Content: The student began with a clear, casual opening, then moved straight into an analysis of Benetton advertisements, their shock value and their tastelessness, giving as an example material on racism which appears to express moral concern, but is used to make large profits. There were thoughtful comments about the economic basis of advertising.

Less good was the lack of any general overview of the aims and rules of advertising conduct. Views were one-sided, showing advertising as a manipulative force.

Tone: Monotonous, lacking variety. Key words were not emphasised and so were lost in the generally flat tone of voice. The student 'dried up' half-way through and lost the thread of what he was saying.

[*Grading*: Level 6/7]

Question 2
Give your views on the nuclear disarmament issue.

Student B
Content: The student gave a clear introduction, sketching in the historical facts. It was a thoughtful analysis, well backed up by facts. The student had a particularly effective range of vocabulary of appropriate style, e.g. 'obliterated, it is said that . . . we live under the shadow of these consequences . . .'

Tone: The student spoke with a soft tone, quietly but audibly. Her tone tended to be monotonous. She was fluent, putting forward her ideas confidently.

[*Grading*: Level 7/8]

Question 3
Give your views on an item currently in the news.

Student C
Content: The student chose to speak on racism. He gave a clear introduction, citing his own personal experience. He hesitated and it seemed he would not continue but eventually he did proceed. He expressed a strong anti-racist attitude, especially with regard to the position of illegal immigrants.

Tone: Confident and forceful speech but with many breaks, leaving the assessor uncertain whether he could continue. Assessor asked questions and he responded effectively but could not get started for quite a while.

[*Grading*: Level 5/6]

Question 4

Provide an interviewing panel with the aims and objectives of a group you represent, together with a simple outline of the project and its cost. Give a 4–5 minute oral submission in support of your bid [for money from the National Lottery]. Be prepared for the panel to question you.

Student D

Content: Well-prepared content with good background knowledge.

   Tone: Fluent and lively speaker, with emphatic body language. Very few hesitations. Student held the attention of the audience very well.

   [*Grading*: Level 8]

Answers
Speaking and listening:
paired and group orals

STUDENT'S RESPONSES AND GRADING: TOPIC 1

(a) With a partner, role-play the following:
    1 the conversation you have with the police officer
    2 the conversation you have with the trouble-makers after the police have left
    3 the conversation you have with your parents when they return home
(b) With your partner, discuss the styles of speech you used in each conversation. What kind of language and expression did you employ in the different situations? Why was the type of spoken English you used appropriate to the situation?

Group I

(a) **1** Student A was effectively fearful and nervous. She stated the situation to the police officer clearly and politely. This was good role-play. Student B was not quite convincing as the police officer. Her manner was too abrupt but the content was good, charging them with a breach of the peace, picking up on alcohol being present. Both showed a good command of suitable registers.

(a) **2** This was an effective conversation between members of the same peer group. Student B was persuasive and forceful but she was not always audible.

(a) **3** Considering the imagined situation, Student A was extremely restrained. She broke role and laughed. She wasn't convincing as a very angry parent. Student B also wasn't quite convincing in the role as the daughter. She should have shown more reaction.

(b) The discussion of the styles of speech used had obviously not been prepared. After a long pause they began and managed quite well. Linguistic analysis was missing as they focused more on emotional content. Rather disappointing.
    [*Grading*: Level 7]

Answers
Reading comprehension: literary text

Geography lesson

1 In each verse two things become clear to the poet. Explain, with reference to the text, what these are.
2 Explain, in your own words, what the title means here.
3 Imagine yourself in a plane. Write about what you see, what you think and what you like or dislike about being there.

1 In the first verse the poet, looking down from the plane, sees the city reduced in size from the distant viewpoint i.e. 'scaled six inches to the mile', and so he is able to see the whole ground plan. When he was on the ground, the city seemed to have been built without a plan and to lack design, being 'haphazard, unplanned and without style', but now he sees that the geographical location has determined the way the city was laid out.

   In verse two he understands, now having an even more distant view so that he can only see the broad physical features, how human settlement has depended on water:

   'it was clear why the country
   had cities where rivers ran...'

   In the final verse he sees the earth as a planet below him and puzzles as to why people on earth can't live together peaceably.
2 The title means that geography will tell you a great deal about why humans live where they do, but it cannot give an answer to why they behave as they do.
3 It is dawn. The plane flying above the city has started on its slow descent to Heathrow. My face is glued to the plane window. The sky is purple like an open wound, the dark blue is lightening up a bit, moving the purple shadows as we hover over the city. I can see a shade of green in the grey of dawn. Through the hanging clouds I can see all of London's face, smiling and shining dimly, as if welcoming me. A pale sun has broken in between the clouds and seems to stripe everything in its light.

   I think about my first renewed contact with the city: the streets, parks, churches, men and women on the street, the grey days, the bright days and feel excited. I feel that something about me has changed since I went away, and nothing will be the same as it was before.

   It is five o'clock on a summer's morning. The city lights stretch out, fading with the end of the night.

   > *Examiner's note* The first two parts of this answer are correct. Part 3 is rather an unusual impressionistic piece of writing. It is relevant, though, and vividly described with some very good phrasing and one striking image: 'the sky is purple like an open wound'. Overall this is an excellent answer.

STUDENT'S ANSWER TO PRACTICE QUESTION

Smokestack Lightning

(a) Look closely at lines 1–30. Explain why Laurence and his family were pleased to move into their new flat in Berwyn Road. What early signs were there that there might be problems for them in their new home?

(b) What do you think about Bert? Referring to the passage, explain what his behaviour tells you about his character.

(a) Laurence and his family were pleased to move to their new home because their old home was becoming too small and cramped.

Laurence, his mother felt, needed a room of his own for studying, and generally because he had to share his room and it was becoming hard to work.

The family would be happier to live in a new house or flat because it would be less cramped, it would, possibly, be nearer to general facilities such as a library, clinic etc. and it could be closer to Laurence's school.

Once they had moved into their new home there were a number of pitfalls which were pointed out in the passage of text. The property looks as if it is being in the middle of being repaired. This could either be because it was in the middle of being repaired or the property had fallen into such a bad state that it looked as if it was being repaired. The front garden obviously had a wall in it which was either being repaired or, again, it had fallen into a state of disrepair.

The wallpaper only covered half of the walls. Before they moved in this should have been remedied. The accommodation was unfurnished and needed to be painted, at least the doors needed to be.

Also, the rent was not too outrageous, as the passage states. It was rare to find this and they should have enquired why it was so low.

(b) Bert had been a professional footballer, presumably earning a fair amount of money. Since an injury which ended his career he has frittered away his money on gambling.

My impression of Bert, from the passage, is that he is a typical workman. All he seems to do is eat, drink, sleep and gamble, with a little bit of work as a builder thrown into his life to make it interesting.

He does not seem to take care either of himself or of his property. This is reflected in the rent he is charging. The passage describes Bert as being a 'lad', and 'incredibly lazy' person and someone who 'never seemed to work'. His behaviour as a gambler tells me that he would rather gamble for a living than work as a builder. The laziness described in the passage also tells me that he would rather not work, but sleep and gamble for a living. Basically, Bert is a lout!

> **Examiner's note** The student's answer to question (a) does try to deal with both parts of the question. Some relevant points are made i.e. they were pleased because their old home was too crowded and Laurence now needs his own room for studying. He also needs to live nearer to the school. The problems stated are those of the disrepair of the house they are moving into. These points are made very repetitiously, though.
>
> In part (b) the student observes several things about Bert i.e. that he once was a professional footballer but now lazes about the house, doing a bit of building work now and again. He gambles and lives in chaotic conditions. Some reference is made to the passage.
>
> Overall, this is of low average competence.

[*Grading*: Level C/D]

4 *Answers*
Reading comprehension: functional text

The Blues

(a) Why is the Blues important in the history of popular music?
(b) What are the main themes of Blues music?
(c) Where would you expect to find a passage like this? Give reasons for your answer.

> (a) The Blues is important in the history of popular music because it was fundamental to the development of modern music e.g. Rock, Folk, Country music are all related to the Blues because the rhythms are basically similar.
>
> (b) The main themes of the Blues are hard times, wretched living conditions, domestic troubles, depression and sadness.
>
> (c) A passage like this could come from a popular history of Jazz for readers who do not yet know much about it. The style is narrative and it seems to explain basic facts about Blues music.

Look carefully at the leaflet *Clayton Castle* and answer the following questions:

(a) What three types of information does it provide for the public? List them.
(b) How is the leaflet set out to make it easy to read?
(c) Find two different styles of writing in the leaflet. Choose examples to support your choice.

> (a) The three types of information are:
>   1 introductory 'blurb', giving a quick, imaginative taste of the attraction of the castle
>   2 historical and architectural facts
>   3 essential information for visitors
>
> (b) It is on one side of a sheet of paper. Each section is separate for clarity. The essential information is in bold print, using capitals, abbreviations and with wide spacing.
>
> (c) The first paragraph is written in relaxed, copywriting style – evocative, imaginative and descriptive. There is use of verbal patterning, alliteration and assonance, such as 'sounds and sights', 'peep into the parlour', 'sweet sounds', 'famous fortress' and also onomatopoeia 'he clatters'. There are descriptive, adjectival phrases, such as 'ghostly Black Duke', 'massive ovens and spits', etc. In contrast, the final paragraph is in telegraphic style – lists, capitals, abbreviations and bold print.

5 Answers
Reading comprehension: media texts

Inferior sunglasses will ruin your eyes

(a) How is the article made appealing to the reader? You may wish to consider the following in your answer:
- ▶ the layout
- ▶ the order in which information is given
- ▶ any other detail you think important

(b) How does the writer use words to interest the reader? Use examples from the article to support what you say.

(a) The article is made appealing to the reader by typical newspaper devices of style. There is a headline in larger and bolder typeface than the rest of the article, which is comparatively short and printed in two columns. The abstract of essential information is given first. Facts and opinions are mixed alternately: there is direct speech: the trading standards officer is quoted as saying 'It is the cheaper sunglasses ... that failed to meet the standards.' It ends with a dramatic warning: 'Wearing sunglasses which don't protect against the sun's ultra violet rays risks causing irreversible eye damage.'

(b) The writer uses language to inform and entertain. Sunglasses, also known as 'shades', are referred to as being part of 'shady deals', a punning reference. There is also some scientific language, such as 'UV protection', 'UV shade number', a 'CE mark' and 'ultra violet rays'.

School meals articles

(a) From Article A, list three worrying findings about food in secondary-school canteens.

(b) In Article B, what arguments are put forward by the Education Boards to defend the School Meals Service? How convincing are these arguments?

(c) How successful is Article A in highlighting the dangers of unhealthy eating? In your answer you should refer to
- ▶ the picture
- ▶ the headlines
- ▶ the words and phrases used
- ▶ the facts presented
- ▶ anything else you feel is important

(a) The three worrying findings about food in school canteens are first that Ulster school children are still being given too much fatty food, with the increased risk of later heart disease. Second, the calories from fat in these foods exceeds the government's upper level by 11%. Third, children do not eat a balanced diet and do not have enough food with iron, calcium or vitamin C.

(b) The Education Board argues that primary schools, which do follow government nutritional standards, were not covered. They deny that food served in secondary schools is unhealthy: only 7% post-primary schools were not members of the Healthy Eating Circle and salad bars were popular in schools. As well as low pricing policies to encourage healthier eating, schools checked their own meals. The Education Board trained staff in how to promote healthier eating. These arguments seem convincing, but the seven primary schools actually make up 20% of the total and the final comment in the article is rather defeatist: 'Society today is very much geared to the consumption of fast foods.'

(c) This article is quite successful. The headline is worrying and eye-catching and the picture is attractive. Louise looks healthy and as if she is enjoying her food. The quoted snatches give the article authenticity. The bomb reference in the heading continues in the first column: 'dietary time-bomb which Northern Ireland school children are sitting on ... gloomy ... death'. Key facts are presented clearly as bullet points. Readers are also helped through the article by sub-headings. Opinions from children, such as Sarah from Antrim and John, a Belfast student, are likely to attract and convince the reader.

Answers
Writing: functional

Diary

STUDENT'S ANSWER TO PRACTICE QUESTION

Write three entries from a teacher's diary.

Mr Green's Diary

Monday 18 October
We're nearly half way through our first term and 5B haven't learned to hand in their Biology assignments yet. Out of a class of 22 only 3 handed it in. I got 'I'm sorry, Sir, my dog ate it.' 'I didn't know we had to hand it in.' This must have been one of my worst days. Luckily John was absent, or it would have been twice as bad. I hope he's absent tomorrow, as well. Today Miss Williams gave me a lift. She kept asking me weird questions.

Tuesday 19 October
I thought I was unlucky yesterday! Today John was back with a vengeance. He threw five spit balls and I got mad so he got up and rushed out of the door.

Wednesday 20 October
Mr Rowe was absent again and I had to take his class in my free period. I think I'm going to leave this job. One boy called me 'Mr Greaser' when he was answering a question. Another got himself beaten up in the back row. What a class! How does Mr Rowe handle them? When I got home I checked my pension details – just in case.

> **Examiner's note** This is a realistic, lively and humorous diary. The layout is correct and the style appropriate. It manages to catch the mind style of a secondary-school teacher and gives vivid accounts of three of his teaching days.

Directed summary

PRACTICE QUESTION

Chaplin's career
Imagine that you have been asked to contribute to an *Encyclopaedia of the Cinema*. Read the following passage and write on two topics: first outline what early movie pictures were like, and second describe Charlie Chaplin's skills as a star. Your article should not be more than 150 words.

EXAMINER'S ANSWER

Early movie pictures were silent. Having no language barriers, they drew in many of the new immigrants, forging a common bond through laughter. Film studios were rough and ready and so were the films themselves. Spontaneous and lacking plot and script, they were produced quickly to make a profit. Gradually, they overcame the view of many that they were low entertainment.

Chaplin transferred his miming and comic skills, learned in popular theatre, to the movies. He invented the role of the little tramp which made him famous. The low status of actors led Chaplin to move on to producing, directing, editing and script-writing. He even wrote film music. Over many years he made a huge contribution to the film industry.

Letter

STUDENT'S ANSWER TO PRACTICE QUESTION

Write Adrian Mole's letter to a problem page.

> 16 February
> 24 South Lane
>
> Dear Problem Page,
> My name is Adrian Mole, and I am thirteen and three-quarters old. These past few weeks I have suffered big problems. As one intellectual to another, I hope you can help me. It all happened like this.
> It was Wednesday when Pandora came to our school. She even sat next to me in Geography. The next day, I fell in love, watching her play netball. She has got long treacle-colour hair. She has also got a good figure.
> I kept showing that I loved her. I let her borrow my blue felt-tip pen and told her her eyes looked like my dog's. Why didn't she notice that I loved her??? The next Friday, me, Pandora and Nigel were at a disco. Nigel started to show off and stuck a safety pin through his ear. We had to take him to the hospital in our car.
> The next day it was official – Nigel and Pandora were going out together!!! I nearly died of shock!!! I don't know what she sees in him. He is a traitor. He knew I was in love with Pandora. How can Nigel do this to me??? How could Pandora do this to me??? How, how, how??? I hate Nigel. I hope he gets squashed like a tomato or gets his brains knocked out when he trips and falls on the pavement.
> It's been three weeks since this happened. Everything has changed. Pandora no longer sits next to me. I even sent her a Valentine's Day card. I didn't get one back though, except from my mother.
> I really need your advice. Please tell me what to do to get her back.
>
> > The one and only
> >
> > Adrian Mole
>
> P.S. Please reply quickly.

> ***Examiner's note*** This is quite a good letter because it has the right tone and style for Adrian Mole. It outlines a problem clearly and in paragraphs. Layout is not entirely right: the address should be a full postal address, the date should follow it and the letter should be addressed to The Editor. The signing off is typically Adrian, however. Notice the 'inventive' punctuation, also typical of Adrian – he would use three ??? or three !!! when only one of each is necessary.

Newspaper article

EXAMINER'S ANSWER TO REVISION ACTIVITY

News item: Ellen's climbing every mountain.

(a) How does the presentation help to get the information across?
(b) Try to work out how the story is organised. Can you find an abstract, orientation and evaluation?
(c) Pick out two sentences and explain how they are typical of newspaper style.

(a) There is a headline in larger print and it is more heavily inked than the main article. The article is in three short paragraphs for quick and easy reading.

(b) The opening paragraph is the abstract, telling the reader just what the news item is about. The next paragraph is the orientation and, as the event has not yet taken place, the article ends by looking forward to what will happen after that event has been undertaken.

(c) The headline is a typical example of a pun or verbal echo much used by tabloid papers: there is play on the song title *Climb Every Mountain* and Ellen Pugh's determination to climb three major peaks in 36 hours. The first sentence of the article has two examples of adjectives placed before the noun: 'A young Clapham woman' and 'a mountaineering spree' – another feature typical of newspaper style.

PRACTICE QUESTION

Many people feel that there is increasing harassment in the workplace. Write an article for a newspaper about a case of harassment which came to court.

STUDENT'S ANSWER TO PRACTICE QUESTION

SAY IT WITH FLOWERS

BRIDE-TO-BE TWENTY-FOUR-YEAR-OLD GLORIA WILSON WON A CLAIM OF HARASSMENT AGAINST HER BOSS, DR STANLEY JONES YESTERDAY.

She claims that her boss constantly plied her with flowers and unwanted gifts. When she asked him to stop, he sacked her. With no job, no money and no hope for the future, pretty Gloria of Southend, Essex, said: 'I still feel very bitter. It would not be fair if he got away with paying me nothing.' Father-of-five, fifty-five-year-old twice married Dr Jones said he has no money to pay pretty Gloria compensation.

> **Examiner's note** Though this is very short it does have some of the features of tabloid reporting. It has a popular saying as a headline, which also makes a key point. The content is a blend of fact and opinion and has some of the direct comments which give these stories the human touch. There is a good deal of premodification of adjectives before the nouns but so extreme as to be parody. There is also triple phrasing: 'no job, no money and no hope for the future'. The article begins with an abstract and an orientation follows. The coda brings the reader up-to-date.

Report

School age raised to 6
Read the information below, and then answer the question that follows.

Imagine that you are the head teacher reporting on the scheme to the Parents' Association. Write two paragraphs from the report, giving:

1 the advantages parents found in the scheme
2 the advantages teachers found in the scheme

End with a recommendation about whether the scheme should be adopted by your own school.

Report to Parents' Association Flower Hill School, Fordham, Herts

HALF-TIME SCHOOLING FOR RECEPTION INFANTS SCHEME

The reasons for implementing the scheme in the county have been discussed above. I now go on to outline the feedback received first from parents whose children have been affected by the scheme and then from teachers in schools where the scheme has been in operation.

Parents, on the whole, considered the scheme advantageous. Analysis of the questionnaire responses showed that 77% of parents found it had some good qualities. Some thought that half-time attendance helped the children to adapt to school more easily, to get used to being away from home and become familiar with a different daily routine. Most mothers thought their children more confident than they would have expected and put it down to the school day being only each morning or afternoon.

Teachers in the schools involved were mostly keen on the scheme, too. The children seemed to be bright and lively and attendance was up, according to one teacher. Children could have the security of working with the same teacher throughout their Reception year.

On the basis of these findings I am seeking your opinions, as parents concerned for the wellbeing of your children and our school, with a view to recommending that we take part in the scheme at Flower Hill, starting from the next school term.

Peter Earnshaw, MA
Head Teacher

Smokestack Lightning
Laurence's mother has applied for a council flat. A housing officer has to visit their house and write a report on their present accommodation. Write the housing officer's report.

Housing Officer's Report: 321 Gothic Towers

This accommodation is only really suitable for one person to live in comfortably. With a family of the size of its present inhabitants I would recommend something larger. The son does not have his own room and at his age he should have a room better suited to his needs as a growing boy. The floorboards in the main room (door adjoining bedroom) have woodworm and consequently are crumbling away. The top right-hand corner of the main bedroom has damp running three-quarters of the way down the wall, the nearest windows do not open properly; one does not open at all. This leads to an extremely pungent smell lingering within the room. The damp could be caused by a leaking roof (confirmation can be sought by further inspection).

Where woodworm, damp and rot are most prominent is where the floorboards are not covered. This is a major patch outside the kitchen door. The uncovered floorboards lead to noise from downstairs not being 'drowned out'. It also leads to a lot of draughts within this area.

The heating system of the block of flats is woefully inadequate; consequently, the family has a 3–bar electric heater in their main room.

The facilities for cooking and storage of food are not good at all. One wall has a mounted cabinet, barely big enough to hold food for a family of this size, and two cabinets under the work surface (one shared with an immersion tank) are also barely enough to hold food and cooking implements for a family of this size.

There are no personal facilities for washing, only the communal bathroom for that floor. Again, this would and should not be acceptable for a family of this size.

> **Examiner's note** This is a realistic report, detailing the inadequacies of the accommodation. It is written in a suitably formal style and has a good deal of the vocabulary associated with a report of this kind. It has a formal heading, but lacks a signature, date and recommendation.
> This is a work of good quality – B grade.

Speech

STUDENT'S ANSWER TO PRACTICE QUESTION

Write two speeches, one in favour and one against the motion that it is a good thing to fight for one's country.

My friends, I see nothing more beautiful than the country we live in. All this could be gone, lost to our aggressor. I have come here today, my friends, to see that this won't happen. I have come to give you a chance to defend your beloved country.

The barbaric enemy may come and slaughter children, people in the streets. Will you stand here and watch them do these unspeakable things? No, of course you won't. You want to fight for the truth and honour of your country. There is nothing more glorious than fighting for your national and your personal pride. So hurry up and sign up to become a proud person, fighting for queen and country.

What will you say to your children when they ask you what you did for your country? What will your family think of you? You are proud of your friends in the army, but what will they think of you? Join today and show them all what you are capable of doing.

When you are walking along the street and see others wearing the queen's uniform, do you feel happy with what you are doing? I think not, so join in and sign up at the recruiting office. Join the country's army. God save the Queen!

My friends, listen to me! I bare the truth to you. That man has just misled you. Do you really think that your going to war is really going to help your loved ones? There is a possibility that you will get killed and where will that leave them? It will leave them mourning your death for the rest of their lives.

He tried to make you feel that it was somehow shameful not to go; he asked you what you would tell your children. Well, if you don't go to war at least you will see your children grow up. What is the point of fighting to kill other ordinary people, just like yourself, with their own children? There is no point, my friends. Go home and fight through the ballot box – you are better off doing that. Jaw is better than War!

> **Examiner's note** These speeches form a pair and in the second some of the issues taken up in the first are answered, though not all e.g. sense of nationalism. A better match could have been achieved. The style, though, is good. It is **declamatory** so that the reader has a sense of hearing the speaking voice. This is achieved partly by directly addressing readers: 'My friends, listen to me!' and partly by the use of many rhetorical questions which echo in the mind and involve the reader in the arguments: 'What is the point of fighting to kill other ordinary people, just like yourself, with their own children?' The final slogan of the second speech (based on Churchill's famous remark 'Jaw, jaw is better than War, war') makes a strong ending.

[*Grading*: Level B]

Answers
Writing:
creative

Descriptive writing

STUDENT'S ANSWER TO PRACTICE QUESTION

Write about a topic of your choice from an unusual point of view.

The clock

Deep down amongst the debris and the dust there is a sudden outburst of activity. Previously inanimate objects come to life, shaking themselves into motion. They moan quietly and their joints creak. Preparations are laboriously made, each one being attended to in order, so that the operation can go ahead satisfactorily.

Way above, the consistent rhythm of normality beats on. The messenger arrives and each individual curls up tightly with anticipation. NOW! The tension is released in one blow, each one driving another until the hammer falls and the clock chimes.

> **Examiner's note** This is an excellent, though short, piece of writing. The action of the clock is minutely described with excellent participles and verbs 'shaking themselves into motion', 'creak', 'each ... curls up tightly', 'tension is released', 'one driving another', 'falls ... chimes'. Careful punctuation controls the pace of the writing – every word is in its right place, and no words fail to contribute to the descriptive account.

Dramatic writing

PRACTICE QUESTION

Interview one of the people in the prereleased booklet *Places* for the radio programme called 'People and Places'. You may like to set out your answer in the form of a drama script.

EXAMINER'S OUTLINE ANSWER

You would need to choose a character presented in the booklet first and think about what kind of life that person may have lived. Then it would be a good idea to list some essential questions that you would like to ask. Remember that if you ask all the questions this is a **directed interview** but you might get a better response by allowing the person more freedom to talk, to tell you things you may not have thought to ask. You should adopt the technique outlined for setting out dramatic text (see pages 43–44). Pay particular attention to how you will open the interview – maybe by introducing the person for your reader – and also how to end it, so that as well as seeming realistic, the piece has a satisfying shape.

Imaginative writing

Write about an imagined experience using the title *Nightmare in Daylight*.

There was no water in the house, so I took a bucket and started walking towards the river to fetch some. It was a nice summer afternoon about three o'clock. The atmosphere was smelling sweet with the scent of the summer flowers. There were a few clouds in the sky, but the warm rays of the sun still cut through the clouds and lighted the house.

Home was on top of a low hill, and the river was just half a mile away. The river ran between steep banks. On one side were wide fields which belonged to my father. As I walked, I was admiring them and I was sort of praying that the rain would keep on falling until the crop had fully grown.

Suddenly, as I was gazing over the field, my eyes captured a weird scene. I saw a girl about the same age as me, walking directly from the graveyard beyond the fields. She looked very strange to me. She walked with her head down, looking at the ground, and eventually she came into the field and started walking towards me.

I got annoyed with her. Why was she walking through my father's field? So I started shouting at her: 'Hey, what are you doing here? Who are you?' There was no reply. The girl still had her face turned away from me. I called again, 'Where are you going?' Still there was no reply, no response. She was now very close to me. I could see that she was wrapped in a dirty tattered coat, which was covered with dry patches of black mud. She herself was very untidy, her hair was full of dust and her legs were marked with scars all over. I became very frightened. My anger had dramatically changed to fear and pity. The girl came quite close to me and stood swaying her shoulders. I couldn't look at her face, and all this time she didn't say a word.

The whole incident must have lasted for about a minute.

Anxiously I looked over my shoulder for help and when I turned back – the girl had vanished. I looked for her footprints on the ground. None. Where did she go? Who was she? Perhaps she was one of my ancestors who had resurrected to reveal something to me. Was it a dream? Obviously it was not. I continued my journey with my knees weak with fear. I kept looking around for the girl but she was not there.

I wanted to tell someone this strange story but somehow I didn't because I felt I would not be believed. For many days I tried to forget that image, but when I sit and think of it, it still stands before me. I will never forget it.

> ***Examiner's note*** This was written by a student who seems to have lived over-seas and probably his first language is not English. The clues to this are the setting of the story – simple countryside, no water, carrying a bucket, fear of ancestors – and the short, separate sentences. The imagined experience itself is very effective, partly because of this simplicity and directness of style. It makes it seem as if the writer were recounting something that really happened. Other ways in which this sense of realism is conveyed is the ending: they don't tell anyone because they think others will not believe it. Also, the idea that the scene is so vivid that it is still remembered is good.

[*Grading*: Level B]

Narrative writing

Write a thriller from the point of view of a third-person narrator while the action is taking place.

In hiding

He walked cautiously to the front door, his eyes scanning the vacant lawn beneath him. He sensed that tonight, something was going to happen. The moon slipped behind a cloud, leaving him in complete darkness. He fumbled at the lock with his key, but as he shifted his weight forwards, the door swung violently open, crashing against the wall stopping its insane swing. The sound echoed in his mind and triggered his heart to begin pounding. It would not rest until he was caught.

Who could possibly know he was here? That question would be recurring many times that evening in his mind, only if he had looked behind him he would have seen a shadow performing prerehearsed moves. If he had looked behind him he might have had a chance.

As he entered, yet again the whirr of silence hit him. It was a silence that a man in hiding must accustom himself to. He was not used to it yet. Using his hands to feel up the sides of the walls, he climbed the stairs, creaking under his weight. He tried to avoid the creaking floorboards by walking in an unusually careful manner, feet pivoted on tiptoes. This only resulted in added noise and added nervousness. He was beginning to become hot. He walked into his make-shift room, drew the curtains and switched on the light.

Everything seemed usual. He looked around the room, secretly hoping to find something that would reinforce his feeling. Nothing! Was he going insane? He frantically began searching from room to room, hoping to find something, anything. He returned to his room, not letting the thoughts escape from his overloaded mind.

He sat down on the bed and opened the freshly bought paper. God, he remembered it had happened yesterday. How long would it be before someone found him? One week – two at the most? He must keep moving around – that's what he had to do. He hurriedly began to throw a few possessions into a small case. Time was his enemy.

Suddenly, he heard a twig snap in the garden below. For a fraction of a second, he froze, wondering whether he had imagined it all. Was his mind playing yet another trick on him? He switched off the light and waited.

While he waited, he prayed that the loud pounding of his heart wouldn't give him away. He was sweating profusely, but dared not wipe the drops in case the slightest movement would tell where he was. His frustration made him desperate to scream. The waiting went on and on.

Suddenly, he heard the creaking of the floor and someone began to climb the stairs. This was his signal to move. His legs seemed too weak to obey his brain. The creaking was coming closer, though the footsteps did not hurry.

Suddenly, he found the power to move. In one swift rush he darted through the open door and bracing himself for the shock he threw himself down to the landing, scrambling up. He had not taken one step when he felt something cold on his wrist. He looked down and saw the handcuff. He was caught. Only then, did he begin to relax.

> **Examiner's note** This story has tremendous tension and final impact. The short terse sentences build up suspense, as does the wish of the character to get some relief from his own inner tension. Little is given away of the reason for his

predicament, but that forces the reader to concentrate on the man's immediate circumstances. Step by step the end draws near – we sense it, yet savour the waiting. This is nearly excellent.

[*Grading*: Level A]

Personal writing

Half-past Two poem
Write about your memories of early school days.

My school days

By the time I had reached the tender age of six, I already excelled in all my studies. I was especially good at mathematics and reading. I did not notice this until the age of six. This was probably because the first year in school was spent having fun with singing and playing.

My father quickly noticed my abilities and encouraged me to push myself. He took on an important role in my studies.

At the age of nine, I had my first conflict in the classroom. The teacher had introduced a system of stars into learning. We received stars for hard work. I was arguing over a trivial matter with a friend when he shouted: 'Shut up, stupid!'

I immediately responded: 'How many stars do you have, then?' I was the child with the most number of stars so far. I knew that I had won the argument. He remained speechless. 'Here, take the silly sharpener then,' I shouted, as if to show my maturity. That week I had other arguments with fellow pupils, mostly deliberately started by myself just so that I could put them down.

I began to push myself harder and harder, so that I could be better than them at work. I saw that other children respected me. I made many friends in this way and worked even harder. Everything was working out right for me. It was a never-ending circle. What had started out as a game evolved into an obsession to attract friends and to succeed in school.

I vividly remember the third year Juniors when I was nine. I was best friends with Jacob. He was also very good at mathematics and during the lesson we would work together as hard as possible, racing through our Maths book. Our friendship seemed to be based on putting each other down. Whenever he made a mistake I would make fun of him, and vice-versa. I realise now that I was not really friends with him at all. Between the ages of six and ten I thrived on winning and did not even realise it.

It was then that I met a person who is now a good friend of mine. He was unlike the rest. Everybody liked him, especially the girls. He had a carefree attitude and did not want to lead. Without trying, though, he became our leader, because of his attitude and self-control. He did not mind failing, being ordered about – he simply shrugged it off. He helped me to realise that leading and winning was not the most important issue in life – life is short and I had to enjoy it.

School is not just a raging war of abilities. It is a process where you can improve your own knowledge. I have adopted his carefree attitude.

> **Examiner's note** This essay does relate to the poem because it shows something important learned at school, and also a maturing process. The writer looks back almost writing of someone else – that detachment is also like the poem. Much of this is straightforward retelling of early experience but the end makes a

general statement, confidently, because it is the product of reflection. Style is not outstandingly good but suitable for the task.

[*Grading*: Level B/C borderline]

Persuasive writing

STUDENT'S ANSWER TO PRACTICE QUESTION

Write in support of an issue that you feel strongly about concerning the rights of school children.

Should corporal punishment be used in schools?

What is corporal punishment? It is whipping and beating for punishment. It is pain inflicted on children, who aren't able to defend themselves, and it is still used in some schools today.

Corporal punishment causes pain to the children and they can't defend themselves. Whatever the teachers do, it is going to cause pain and the children can do nothing to get back — only accept the pain and keep quiet. If the child bursts out in defence, this could lead to another punishment, probably worse than the first. Corporal punishment teaches children to keep quiet about their feelings, so later in life, when the child has bigger problems he or she may keep feelings inside and so become depressed, maybe leading to the use of drugs or something much worse. Being hit and abused during childhood may lead to problems later in life.

The punishment can be used in the line of teaching respect, but the child involved may only learn to dislike the teacher and hold a grudge, so behaviour becomes worse. To have corporal punishment as the only deterrent means that the children will come back for more.

Corporal punishment is humiliating. Being hit and scolded in front of other people is embarrassing. Humiliating or embarrassing the child is a way of increasing the child's dislike towards the teacher. This does not help, especially if the child is domineering and influences the thoughts and views of other children; then any respect for the teacher is gone.

Some teachers simply use the punishment for survival in a tough school. They may not like the idea, but have to hit the children to show them they will use the punishment — they use corporal punishment to prove a point.

Take, for example, a scene in the movie *Kes*. Some boys are being punished for smoking, and the headmaster says he will continue to hit people until something better comes along. This means he knows it won't stop the boys smoking but he has no other form of punishment to deal out that the boys will remember.

In earlier times in schools there was a saying:

'Learning that is not willingly sought
With the rod must needs be taught.'

This is a threat, saying if children are lazy or do not want to work, they will be hit until they want to learn. This is clearly the wrong way to go about education. Children need to learn because they want to, not because they have to. They may oppose, become stubborn and simply refuse to work. No amount of beating is going to give children the inspiration to learn.

The law in Europe now says that it is wrong to beat children but it still goes on in some schools. Corporal punishment may sometimes get results but it can also backfire and cause even more problems. The way to instil discipline and respect is through reasoning and talking to pupils, rather than to use violence.

Examiner's note The student puts forward several points to support his or her view here. He/she also considers one or two ideas from a different standpoint. Organisation of content is haphazard, though, and a bit repetitive. Some sentence structures are careless, e.g. 'The punishment can be used in the line of teaching respect'. The conclusion is clear and strong.

[*Grading*: Level C/D borderline]

8 *Answers*
Spelling, handwriting and presentation

STUDENT'S WRITING DURING EXAM CONDITIONS

This typical scheme of assessment allows for a mark out of ten to be awarded for the script overall, the key element being the degree of consistency shown. So, if you misspell a simple word here and there, but in general your work is very good, the few errors will not weigh too much. Also it would be very unfair for a student who writes very simply but with no errors to gain the same mark as one who uses a complex and full vocabulary and misspells a few difficult words. These matters are also taken into account.

Here is a typical grading scheme:

Mark	Criteria
1–2	A limited range of words will be spelled in a recognisable way.
3	A reasonable range of simple words will be used and often spelled correctly.
4	Students will attempt some more complex words, containing mainly suffixes and prefixes, and will often spell such words correctly, but with a large number of errors overall.
5	Students will often show the capacity to spell correctly words with such features as doubled consonants, but will not do so consistently, and writing will contain a regular sprinkling of errors.
6	Students will often show the capacity to spell some relatively complex words, including those in groups with related spellings. Their writing will contain a significant number of errors, though substantial sections may well be error-free.
7	Students will spell correctly most words used, including, for example, some borrowed from other languages. Their errors will be fairly infrequent (perhaps including mistakes with commonly misspelled words such as 'necessary', 'accommodate' and 'definite').
8	Students will spell correctly almost all words used, and the range of these words will be fairly wide and appropriate. Errors will be infrequent.
9	Students' spelling will be extremely accurate, with a wide range of words tackled correctly and only occasional slips in attempts at ambitious words creating errors.
10	Students' spelling will be of exceptionally high quality, accuracy extending to include words selected from an extensive range of vocabulary. Errors will be practically non-existent.

Examiner's notes on student's work

1 This student's work falls between categories 2 and 3 above. The words used are mostly simple and correct, and more complex words, such as 'recycled', have been copied from the set passage, mostly correctly. It is disturbing that the student still confuses capitals and small case letters, though this is partly the result of lack of control of handwriting. The small case 'i' is a very basic error. [*Final award*: 2]

2 The student uses a range of words confidently and mostly correctly. The mis-spelling of 'they' is basic; it may be a slip or an aspect of dialect. Overall, though, this is reasonably competent work.
[*Final award*: 6]

3 This student writes fluently with a complex vocabulary and the work is error-free.
[*Final award*: 10]

part IV
Timed practice papers
with answers

In this part of the book we suggest that you start to practise writing timed answers, just as you will have to do in the actual exam.

Each paper lasts for two hours. Set an alarm clock to ring when the time is up.

Try to leave yourself five minutes before the end of essay-type questions so that you can check over your work and self-correct. Aim to complete the papers – remember that unfinished papers are those which are most likely to fail.

TIMED PRACTICE PAPER 1

Practice Paper A: Chapters 3, 6 and 7

Question Paper for reading comprehension: literary text, and functional and creative writing

ENGLISH PAPER 1   2 HOURS

Answer all four questions in Section A, and one from Section B

Section A

This section deals with **reading skills**.

Read the passage carefully and answer **all four questions** in this section.

Characters
Travis: Head teacher
Kyle: Fifth-year boy
Shearer: PE teacher

Mr Travis, the head teacher of an inner-city school, is at his wits' end. The building is falling apart. Truancy and vandalism are problems, and members of staff, unable to cope with the pressure, are repeatedly off sick.

Then, to top it all, Mr Shearer brings Kyle, a fifth-year student, to see him. He has been accused of stealing money from the changing-room. Kyle is the last person Travis wants to see. He regards Kyle as a failure. Kyle thinks school is unimportant and boring. His main interest is out of school – at 'Fun City'...

[Head teacher's study. Travis, the head teacher, is doing press-ups in his shirt sleeves in the middle of the room. There is a knock on the door. Travis stops, then puts on his jacket and sits at his desk. He picks up a sheet of paper.]

Travis: Come in!
[There is a pause then Kyle, a fifth-year boy, shuffles in closely followed by Mr Shearer, a young PE teacher. Shearer is dressed in track suit and trainers, Kyle in ripped jeans, worn trainers, army surplus combat jacket with names of pop groups felt-tipped on it and a woollen hat. Mr Shearer looks annoyed, the boy sullen and angry.]
Travis: [still panting from his exercise] What is it Mr Shearer?
Shearer: I'd like you to have a word with Kyle if you would, Mr Travis.
        There's been some money stolen from the gym changing-room...
Kyle: Well, it wasn't me! I didn't take it!

continued

continued

Shearer: Of course you did. It couldn't have been anybody else.

Kyle: It must have been, 'cos I didn't do it!

Travis: Stop shouting lad! Who do you think you're talking to? [Then to *Shearer*] Can't Mr Franklin deal with this? I'm extremely busy.

Shearer: He's teaching. He's had to fill in for somebody.

Travis: Don't tell me someone else is off sick! They're dropping like flies. No stamina, that's the trouble. [He raises his arms and presses them back three times in a shoulder-stretching exercise.] What about Mrs Sherwood, isn't she available?

Shearer: She's not in school. She's had to take a girl to hospital.

Travis: [Alarmed] Why, what's happened?

Shearer: A door came off its hinges. She got trapped underneath.

Travis: [Pointing at the ceiling] Yes, and I shall be the next casualty. Just look at those cracks. The whole place is falling apart around our ears.

Shearer: What about the showers in the changing-rooms? Not only is there no hot water; but when a boy turned them on the other day he got an electric shock!

[*Kyle* tries hard not to grin at this news.]

Travis: Perhaps you should try switching on the lights, see if you get any hot water out of the sockets. [Pauses while he does an exercise, linking his fingers and pulling hard] It's the cuts. When somebody gets killed, they might call a halt. [Then, noticing *Kyle* trying to hide a grin] What are you smirking at, Kyle?

Kyle: Nothing, Sir.

Travis: I don't suppose there's much chance of you getting electrocuted in the showers, judging by the state of you. And take that hat off. It's not that cold in school.

Shearer: You should come down to the gym. It's like a freezer in there.

Travis: Economy, Mr Shearer. That's the key word these days. Look at this lot ... [He picks up a wad of papers from his desk] If I took all the reminders I receive from County Hall down to the boiler room, they'd produce enough heat for the boys to walk around the school in swimming trunks.

[*Kyle* takes off his hat. His head is completely shaven except for a coloured strip of hair down the centre.]

Travis: [Pause, then slowly with great feeling] Who on earth gave you that?

Kyle: [Puzzled] What?

Travis: That thing! That ... [lost for words] That thing on top of your head!

Kyle: [Grinning and stroking his hair proudly] Mario's, the hairdressers in town.

Travis: You mean you actually paid to have it done?

Kyle: Well, he's not going to do it free, is he?

[*Shearer* keeps his head down, trying hard to hide his amusement]

Travis: [Walking round *Kyle* and shaking his head in disbelief] You should be struck off the roll. [Pause] And what about your parents? What do they say about it?

Kyle: [Shrugging] They're not bothered. Anyway, it's my hair.

Travis: I'm glad it is, lad. If it was mine I'd blow my brains out. And even if your parents approve, I certainly don't. That hairstyle is totally unacceptable. I'm trying to run a respectable school here.

[*Travis* sits down at his desk, puts his palms together in front of his chest and presses until he is red in the face.]

continued

continued

Travis: Now then, tell me what happened, Mr Shearer.

Shearer: Well, we were out on the field and Kyle said he wanted to go to the toilet.

Kyle: You're not blaming me...

[The telephone rings on *Travis*'s desk. He picks it up.]

Travis: Yes... They were doing what...? In RE? Well, tell them to report to my room at twelve o'clock. I'm busy at the moment. [He replaces the telephone receiver] Riot in Room 15 by the sound of it. Whatever next? [Pause] Sorry about that Mr Shearer, you were saying...

Shearer: Well, I gave him the key to the changing-room. We carried on with the game and a few minutes later he came back. Then when they were getting changed at the end of the lesson, Weston said that he'd had five pounds stolen out of his pocket.

Kyle: Well, I didn't take it.

Travis: [Ignoring him] Are you sure Weston wasn't making it up?

Shearer: No, you could tell. He was genuinely upset. His mother had given it to him to get some shopping on his way home from school.

Travis: Perhaps he'd lost it.

Shearer: He says he checked his pockets before he went out on to the field.

Travis: Well, it's obvious where it's gone then, isn't it? It's an open and shut case.

Kyle: I haven't got it.

Travis: Who has, then? It can't have vanished into thin air.

Kyle: How do I know?

Travis: Look, lad, it's obvious. And I'm telling you, if we don't get that money back I shall turn the matter over to the police.

Kyle: [Pause] You can do what you like, I didn't take it.

Travis: You know what'll happen, don't you, if the police get involved? With your record you could be in serious trouble.

[*Kyle* does not answer.]

Shearer: I've promised him, Mr Travis, that if we get the money back it won't go any further. I don't want to see him get into any more trouble and I'm sure you don't.

Travis: Of course not.

Kyle: How can I, when I haven't got it?

Shearer: [Almost pleading] Come on, Tony. I'll give it quietly back to Weston and nobody will hear any more about it. All he wants is his money back.

Travis: Have you searched him?

Shearer: I made him empty his pockets. But he's hardly going to go walking about with it on him, is he? It could be anywhere.

Travis: [Losing patience] Kyle! Where is it?

Kyle: I've no idea.

Travis: Come on, lad. It's obvious. It must be you.

Kyle: Prove it.

Travis: I don't have to prove it. I know! I'm telling you here and now that you're not leaving this room until I get that money back. I don't care if you've to stay till nine o'clock tonight.

[There is a pause while *Travis* and *Shearer* look at *Kyle*, who shows no reaction to this threat.]

Travis: [Looking at his watch] You'd better get back to your class, Mr Shearer. Just leave him to me now.

Now answer questions 1–4 which follow.

1 What has Kyle been accused of doing?
2 What do you think it would be like to go to Kyle's school? You should support what you write by referring to details in the passage about the school buildings, the pupils, the staff, and anything else you think is important.
3 What do you learn about Kyle? You should support what you write by referring closely to the passage. You might like to include details about his appearance, his attitude to school, his behaviour, and anything else you think is important.
4 Is Mr Travis a good headmaster? You should support your views by referring closely to the details in the passage about his relationships with pupils, his relationships with staff, his attitude to his work and anything else you think is important.

Section B
This section deals with **writing skills**.

Answer one question from this section

Either
5 Write about what takes place in the staff room at lunch time, as a one-act play. Shearer has a discussion with other members of staff about Kyle, the head teacher and the problems of the school.
As well as their conversation, you may wish to include some comments and stage directions like those used by the writer. These should help you to show the thoughts and feelings of the characters.

Or
6 Imagine you are a parent of a pupil at Travis's school. You have become very concerned after a recent Parents' Evening and after listening to what your child has told you about the school.
Write a letter to Mr Travis in which you make your feelings known. Outline problems and suggest how the school could be improved. (**NICCEA**)

OUTLINE ANSWERS

1 Stealing money.
2 **A basic answer** will report some facts about the school. Comments will be of a simple, general nature. A few examples will be used.
An average answer will make some comment about what it would be like to attend the school, noting the more obvious facts relating to the state of the buildings, the morale of the staff and the behaviour of the pupils. There will be a range of examples.
A good answer will show an appreciation of the question by making a range of appropriate inferences about the effects of decaying buildings, the low morale of staff, limited leadership and the low motivation of students.
Reference may be made to some or all of the following:
▶ Building falling apart
▶ Truancy
▶ Vandalism
▶ Staff unable to cope – often off sick
▶ Door came off hinges – girl trapped underneath
▶ Cracks in ceiling
▶ No hot water in showers
▶ Faulty electrics

- ▶ Lack of heating
- ▶ Cuts blamed
- ▶ Riots in RE
- ▶ Staff appear uninterested in students

3   **A basic answer** will report facts about Kyle. Comments will be of a simple nature. Some listing, particularly about his appearance, is likely.

An average answer will draw some inferences from the facts about Kyle. A range of examples should be used. His attitude to school and to those in authority may be noted.

A good answer will show an appreciation of Kyle's character by making a range of appropriate inferences about Kyle. Some of the following may be used:

- ▶ His attitude to school
- ▶ Hatred of Travis
- ▶ Statements made by his dress
  - – defensive behaviour
  - – sense of humour
  - – disregard for those in authority
- ▶ His concern over his past record
- ▶ Frustration at not being believed

Reference may be made to some or all of the following:

- ▶ Appearance
  - – ripped jeans
  - – worn trainers
  - – combat jacket – pop star names in felt-tip
  - – woollen hat
  - – looks sullen and angry
  - – Mohican haircut – coloured
  - – proud of haircut
- ▶ Hates Travis
- ▶ Thinks school unimportant and boring
- ▶ Main interest is 'Fun City'
- ▶ Defensive
- ▶ Not believed by Travis or Shearer
- ▶ No respect for Travis or Shearer – shouts
- ▶ Tries to hide grin later
- ▶ Lack of parental control
- ▶ Lack of concern for parents
- ▶ Concerned about police involvement
- ▶ Has a past record
- ▶ Called Tony
- ▶ Gives no reaction to Travis' threats
- ▶ Aggressive
- ▶ Any other relevant points

4   **A basic answer** will report some facts about Travis. Comments will be of a simple subject nature.

An average answer will show a clearer ability to express valid opinions about Travis. Comments will be supported by a range of examples drawn from the passage. Some appreciation of the difficulties faced by the head teacher and his reaction to them may be expressed. Some indication of his ineffectiveness as a leader/professional may be explored.

A good answer will exploit the material more fully. Opinions should be supported by close reference to the text, using appropriate examples. Your answer may refer to a number of aspects of Travis's character. Some of the following may be noted: his infatuation with exercise training, his lack of concern for his staff and school, his dislike of the students, particularly Kyle, the importance he places on impression. His ineffectiveness as a leader/professional may be explored, as may his reluctance to accept responsibility.

Reference may be made to some or all of the following:
- ▶ At his wits' end
- ▶ Concerned about the school falling apart
- ▶ Can be sarcastic and makes light of problems
- ▶ Kyle the last person he wants to see
- ▶ Regards Kyle as a failure – hates him
- ▶ Exercise freak
- ▶ Hypocrite – wanting to make a good impression, not taking his duties seriously
- ▶ Claims to be 'extremely busy'
- ▶ Not wanting to accept responsibility/lazy (passing on issues to Mr Franklin/ Mrs Sherwood; blaming 'cuts')
- ▶ Contempt for staff
- ▶ Alarmed when girl gets hurt
- ▶ Sarcastic with Kyle
- ▶ Makes excuses for poor working conditions
- ▶ Traditional – no sympathy with youth culture/fads
- ▶ Some concern for outside opinion – respectable school
- ▶ Does not respond to emergencies – riot in Room 15, no response until twelve o'clock!
- ▶ Poor view of most students – distrusts Weston
- ▶ Holds past over Kyle
- ▶ Makes threats he can't/won't carry out
- ▶ Any other relevant points must be credited

Practice Paper B: Chapters 4 and 6

Question Paper for reading comprehension: functional text and functional writing

ENGLISH PAPER 2   2 HOURS

Read the following passage and answer Question A and either B (i) or B (ii)

Why do we need trees?

We all enjoy the beauty of trees and their cooling shade but we need them for a more important reason: human life itself depends on trees. They have a basic part to play in preserving the environment we live in, the land itself. They also clean the air we breathe by replenishing the oxygen supply. Trees, too, act as a buffer against noise pollution.

We will consider each of these vital roles in turn. Firstly, the globe was originally covered with trees. As the human race grew, so the trees lessened. Forests were in the way of human expansion: trees were cut down to clear land for farming, to provide timber for our needs. So human beings set about destroying the forests and, more often than not, failing to replant them. No thought was taken about future generations, and now we are paying the price.

But what is the price? Well, you could think of a tree as a pump. Every day it removes about four hundred litres of water from the soil. If that ceases to happen the water and sub-soil salt rise and damage, even destroy surface vegetation. Salt gets into rivers and streams and there is further damage done.

Secondly, trees affect the purity of the air we breathe. Dust, ash, ozone, unhealthy chemicals are largely filtered out by plants. Trees absorb carbon dioxide from the atmosphere, combine it with water and convert it into sugars which they use for growth. During the process the leaves give off oxygen which humans need to survive. Tests have shown that every ton of timber enriches the air vastly by producing oxygen and removing approximately one and a half times as much carbon dioxide.

Thirdly, with the growth of cities and the increasing popularity of road transport there has been an increase in noise. Trees help to break up sound. Every dense clump of trees reduces noise by a considerable degree. Of course, they add greatly to the beauty of our world, also. Would you rather face a four-lane motorway or an avenue of poplars?

So, if you want a a better environment, cleaner air, less noise pollution and a more beautiful world around you – plant some trees.

A Explain how trees help to keep the land and streams in a healthy condition and affect the air we breathe. [*30 marks*]

EITHER

B (i) Write a leaflet for your local Plant a Tree week, bringing out clearly the advantages of trees for the environment.

OR

B (ii) You have heard that the local council is planning to cut down a line of mature trees alongside a stretch of railway near your home because leaves from the trees fall on the track during autumn. Write a letter of protest, taking into account the need for rail safety but explaining why you feel that the trees should remain. (**London**)

OUTLINE ANSWERS

A **A basic answer** would make one or two simple points in random order.
An average answer would distinguish between the beneficial effects trees have on the land, streams and air, giving maybe one example for each.
A good answer would distinguish between the beneficial effects trees have on the land, streams and air, giving most of the points listed below.

1 Beneficial effects of trees on the land:
  ▶ Trees act as pumps preventing water from rising and bringing salt to the surface of the land where it will harm plant growth
2 Beneficial effects of trees on the streams
  ▶ Trees prevent salt from the soil flowing into rivers and streams and causing pollution
3 Beneficial effects of trees on the air
  ▶ Trees absorb pollutants including carbon dioxide and give off oxygen which we need to breathe

B (i) **A basic answer** here would just include one or two ideas, for example about trees being beautiful and cutting down noise, paying little attention to style or layout.
An average answer here would include many more ideas such as the beauty of trees, their beneficial effect on the air and the land, and their increasing value in cutting down noise pollution. Style would take account of a public audience and there would be some attempt at a suitable layout, with a heading and short paragraphs.
A good answer would include all the points above, attempt to interest the reader by a direct and clear style and take care with layout and presentation. There would be a banner headline, bullet points, different sizes of writing and so on.

B (ii) **A basic answer** here would make a few points about the benefits of trees and probably spend too long on the personal situation of the writer, such as having a home near the line. There may be some form of address or greeting, but these would be sketchy.

An average answer would mention the need for passenger safety, acknowledging the risk of leaves on the track, but make points about the greater value of trees as buffers against noise and as beautifying the environment. There would be an address, a form of greeting and a signature. Style would be clear but not particularly appropriate.

A good answer would offer a balanced argument, taking into account the needs for safety on the railway but also putting forward a persuasive case for the needs of the local community in terms of trees helping with less noise, a lovely environment, a screen from the railway, and so on. Style would be formal and so would layout: there would be a full address, a formal greeting and a signing off.

No. of weeks before the exams	Date: Week commencing	MONDAY	TUESDAY	WEDNESDAY	THURSDAY	FRIDAY	SATURDAY	SUNDAY
9								
8								
7								
6								
5								
4								
3								
2								
1								

LONGMAN EXAM PRACTICE KITS

REVISION PLANNER

Titles Available –

GCSE	A-LEVEL
Biology	Biology
Business Studies	British and European
Chemistry	Modern History
English	Business Studies
French	Chemistry
Geography	Economics
German	French
Higher Maths	Geography
Information	German
Systems	Mathematics
Mathematics	Physics
Physics	Psychology
Science	Sociology

There are lots of ways to revise. It is important to find what works best for you. Here are some suggestions:

- try testing with a friend: testing each other can be fun!
- label or highlight sections of text and make a checklist of these items.
- learn to write summaries – these will be useful for revision later.
- try reading out loud to yourself.
- don't overdo it – the most effective continuous revision session is probably between forty and sixty minutes long.
- practise answering past exam papers and test yourself using the same amount of time as you will have on the actual day – this will help to make the exam itself less daunting.
- pace yourself, taking it step by step.

Getting Started — *Begin on week 12*

Use a calendar to put dates onto your planner and write in the dates of your exams. Fill in your targets for each day. Be realistic when setting the targets, and try your best to stick to them. If you miss a revision period, remember to re-schedule it for another time.

Get Familiar — *Weeks 12 and 11*

Identify the topics on your syllabuses. Get to know the format of the papers – time, number of questions, types of questions. Start reading through your class notes, coursework, etc.

Get Serious — *Week 10*

Complete reading through your notes – you should now have an overview of the whole syllabus. Choose 12 topics to study in greater depth for each subject. Allocate two topic areas for each subject for each of the next 6 weeks

No. of weeks before the exams	Date: Week commencing	MONDAY	TUESDAY	WEDNESDAY	THURSDAY	FRIDAY	SATURDAY	SUNDAY
12								
11								
10